Breakthrough Business Analysis

IMPLEMENTING AND SUSTAINING A VALUE-BASED PRACTICE

Breakthrough Business Analysis

IMPLEMENTING AND SUSTAINING A VALUE-BASED PRACTICE

KATHLEEN B. HASS

MANAGEMENTCONCEPTSPRESS

MANAGEMENTCONCEPTS PRESS

8230 Leesburg Pike, Suite 800
Tysons Corner, VA 22182
(703) 790-9595
Fax: (703) 790-1371
www.managementconcepts.com

Portions of this book have been adapted with permission from:

- *Business Analysis Center of Excellence: The Cornerstone of Business Transformation* by
  Kathleen Hass, PMP, with Richard Avery and Terry Longo. © 2007 by Management
  Concepts, Inc.
- *The Enterprise Business Analyst: Developing Creative Solutions to Complex Business
  Problems* by Kathleen B. Hass. © 2011 by Management Concepts, Inc.
- *Managing Complex Projects: A New Model* by Kathleen B. Hass, PMP. © 2009 by
  Management Concepts, Inc.

Printed in the United States of America

Library of Congress Control Number: 2014938684

ISBN 978-1-56726-464-7

eISBN 978-1-56726-465-4

To Patrick, my first-born son, who taught me that there are many ways to soar, from a submariner to an IT professional.

About the Author

Kathleen (**Kitty**) **Hass** is the world's leading expert in strategic business analysis (BA) and complex project management. She has written dozens of articles and nine books, including the renowned series *The Business Analysis Essential Library; The Enterprise Business Analyst: Developing Creative Solutions to Complex Business Problems;* and *Managing Project Complexity: A New Model,* which was awarded the Project Management Institute's David I. Cleland Literature Award.

Kitty is a professor of strategic business analysis and project management practices at Villanova University and a keynote speaker at conferences around the world. She is a director on the International Institute of Business Analysis (IIBA) board and is on the BA advisory boards for Capella University and the University of California, Irvine.

Contents

Foreword

When I began my career as a business analyst (BA) in the 1980s, the role of the BA was coupled with that of computer programmer. After completing my undergraduate degree in management information systems, I was employed under the job title "programmer/analyst"—with the emphasis on programmer. The duties, responsibilities, tasks, and deliverables of my role as programmer were fairly clear, and my performance was easily measured—the code either worked or it didn't.

From compiling source code using punch cards and the first Apple personal computer, to the worldwide web and beyond, I have witnessed a lot of positive change and growth in the business analysis profession. The role has been joined with testing, training, and frequently project management. In many of my clients' organizations, individuals wear multiple hats, for example, performing the roles of BA, project manager, and tester. The BA role has evolved and merited its stand-alone job title.

Now more than ever, quality training is available to help BAs learn techniques. Excellent guides describe the work a BA performs and provide models for business analysis capability maturity. Automated tools significantly enhance productivity. Yet many business analysts still find themselves having to prove their value in the organization.

Performing business analysis is challenging in a global integrated economy. As industry trail-blazer Kathleen Hass explains in *Breakthrough Business Analysis: Implementing and Sustaining a Value-Based Practice*, it's all about adding measurable business value. This book can help business analysts and business analysis practice leads succeed in a solution-focused environment. Kathleen provides a wealth of wisdom and insight for determining organizational readiness and then implementing and sustaining a value-based BA practice.

You can apply the concepts in this book in organizations of all sizes and industries. Use it as a reference. Read it once, and read it again and again. Each time you read this book, you'll come to understand the depth of the advice Kathleen presents. You'll also benefit from the experiences shared by the book's contributors.

I'm excited for the future as business analysts continue to stand out in organizations as strategic assets. *Breakthrough Business Analysis* will likely lead the 21st century as a definitive treatise on implementing and sustaining value-based business analysis practices.

—Roxanne Miller
President, Requirements Quest
Author, *The Quest for Software Requirements*

Preface

All around the globe, business leaders are engaged in the practice of business analysis (BA). Regrettably, in far too many instances, the business results are marginal at best. The myriad reasons for this limited success include the following:

- The stubbornly durable view of business analysis as an administrative endeavor vs. a value-creating strategy execution framework

- Bottom-up, project-by-project implementation vs. systematic, holistic approaches

- A singular focus on requirements management vs. a strategic focus on innovation and value.

This book provides a rational framework for implementing a BA practice successfully in an organization—a BA practice that is strategically positioned and value-based. Realizing the positive impacts of a value-based BA practice could very well mean the difference between success and failure for businesses negotiating 21st century challenges.

Most of us think of business analysis as comprising the capabilities needed to manage requirements at the project level. To succeed at this level, a basic BA methodology needs to be in place, containing elements that will enable delivering projects on time, on budget, and with the full scope of features and functions that meet business objectives. However, studies show that we are successful less than 40 percent of the time at meeting project time, cost, and scope estimates. In most cases, we don't measure the business benefits of the new business product, service, or capability, so we actually don't know if the project adds real business benefits.

WHAT IS VALUE-BASED BUSINESS ANALYSIS?

Value-based business analysis involves leadership, imagination, inspiration, and ingenuity in addition to the more tactical requirements-management capabilities at the project level. Project-level BA practices are still needed, but their roles are changing significantly as integrated tools replace many BA tasks.

Value-based business analysis centers on strategy execution, world-class enterprise capabilities, and delivery of innovative products and services. It encompasses, but is very different from, typical business analysis activities aimed at defining and managing requirements.

Sometimes referred to as enterprise business analysis, value-based BA practices demand more mature methods that embrace complexity, adaptive change, innovation, and the power of teams. Higher BA maturity levels are directly correlated to more effective business alignment of projects, higher quality business solutions, increased customer value, increased creativity and innovation, and enhanced business benefits resulting from the implementation of new business solutions.

Value-based BA practices concentrate on several areas that have been woefully inadequate in managing business change initiatives:

- Methods and tools that are lean and iterative to accelerate delivery of value

- Leadership that welcomes diversity of perspectives and fosters experimentation, creativity, disruptive change, and breakthrough processes and products

- Teams that are expert, collaborative, and high-performing

- Thinking that is global, holistic, and strategic and that leverages complexity to cultivate creativity

- Solutions that are innovative and competitive

- Decision-making that is based on value to customers and wealth to bottom the line.

HOW THIS BOOK IS STRUCTURED

In the Introduction, we present a framework for implementing and sustaining a value-based BA practice. The three parts of the book then correspond to the framework, which comprises three phases:

1. The initial readiness phase: "Is our organization ready?"

2. The subsequent implementation phase: "How do we build the BA practice?"

3. The ongoing sustainability phase: "How do we institutionalize and continue to improve BA practices?"

PART I: READINESS

In this part, we spend some time assessing the readiness of your organization to support a new or different BA practice, answering the question, "Is your organization ready?" Readiness is defined as having the following elements in place:

- A business case describing the value and cost of implementing a mature BA practice

- An executive sponsor who is accountable for the business benefits derived from an effective BA practice

- A steering committee to guide the BA practice evolution

- A respected and influential BA practice lead.

In Chapter 1 we provide an approach to determining whether your organization is ready to implement more sophisticated BA practices. We examine the culture of your organization, how to develop a strong case for your proposed value-based BA practice working at strategic levels, and how to establish a lean, effective governance structure for the practice.

In Chapter 2 we provide information for you, the BA manager/BA practice lead, and senior BAs to determine if you are ready to assume a leadership role in implementation of the value-based BA practice. We discuss business and politics in your organization, exploring your power, credibility, and influence. We present the idea of using a political management plan to build your network of supporters and to assess environmental risks. We also discuss the need for an influential BA practice lead at the helm.

PART II: IMPLEMENTATION

In this part we explore the activities involved in implementing a new or advancing an existing BA practice. According to our framework, the implementation phase answers the question, "How do we build the BA practice?" Implementation consists of:

- A customized BA center of excellence (BACOE)

- A capable BA team

- Effective lean BA practice standards.

Chapter 3 addresses getting the structure of your practice right during the start-up phase. We first examine the types of models that can provide a home for the BA practice—a department that is accountable and responsible for building and sustaining effective BA practices.

In Chapter 4 we present a groundbreaking approach to building a capable BA team. We lay out a step-by-step process for determining the level of capability needed on your team, based on the complexity profile of current and anticipated assignments. Today, BAs are mostly project-focused, creating and managing requirements artifacts. However, to become a valuable corporate asset, BAs need to become holistic thinkers who are strategically focused, concentrating on innovative solutions to complex business problems.

In Chapter 5 we acknowledge that an organization is only as good as its practices. New/improved BA processes need to fit with the organization's existing processes and methods. We also explore the opportunity to use tools to help educate BAs on the practices, integrate and manage requirements knowledge and artifacts, and incorporate engineering information into the BA artifacts used to build the solution.

PART III: SUSTAINABILITY

In this part, we discuss important strategies to sustain and continually improve your BA practices, answering the question, "How do we institutionalize and continue to improve BA practices?" We offer suggestions on critical success factors.

Chapter 6 discusses the need to run your BA practice like a business. We include suggestions regarding the key elements of a successful business.

Chapter 7 suggests approaches to measuring the effectiveness of your BA practice. We propose methods to demonstrate value through project performance, quality performance, quality processes, and quality reviews.

Chapter 8 discusses the need for business analysts and the BA practice as a whole to focus on innovation. We discuss innovation from several different perspectives: what creative teams look like, how to become a creative leader, and how to measure creativity.

Chapter 9 focuses the need for us to change the way we do projects. It includes shifting our focus, specifically how we view and use business cases, identify innovative opportunities, lead projects, execute projects, collaborate, deploy new solutions, measure project success, and sustain the new vision of project work.

Chapter 10 presents approaches to executing a well-planned strategic communication approach. We explore how to craft strategic messages that are customized and memorable, and how to drive decision-making with executive teams.

Chapter 11 explores how to transform your BA team from an effective group to a high-performing team. We examine how to build and sustain a high-performing team, how to lead teams, and the characteristics of high-performing teams. Managing virtual teams is also discussed.

CONCLUSION

In the conclusion, we acknowledge that world-class BAs must stay ahead of trends both within business analysis and within their industry. We explore the business analysis approaches and trends that are taking root around the globe.

PUTTING IT ALL TOGETHER

WHAT DOES THIS MEAN FOR THE BUSINESS ANALYST?

Traditional BA jobs are going away and are not coming back. BA tools are growing up, and typical BA tasks are being automated and commoditized. Instead of being regarded as documenters, BAs will be sought out to focus on strategy, innovation, and leadership.

As a BA working at the project level, work with your organization to adopt a contemporary requirements management tool that supports business analysis of the future. Strive to become expert at collaboration, creativity, innovation, and value realization. Then, you will truly be a vital asset to your organization.

WHAT DOES THIS MEAN FOR THE BA MANAGER/PRACTICE LEAD?

The BA practice lead is emerging as the champion of a value-based, breakthrough BA practice. This encompasses transforming the role of the BA practitioner as well as the roles of all other stakeholders involved in executing successful BA practices, including project managers, solution developers, business managers, business owners, product owners, technologists, architects, and sometimes suppliers and partners.

To implement a value-based BA practice, you will need to build relationships with and influence virtually everyone in your organization. The role of BA practice lead is perhaps the most exciting leadership function in organizations today. So, don't blink, don't hesitate, or you might miss out!

—**Kathleen B. (Kitty) Hass, PMP**

kittyhass@comcast.net

www.kathleenhass.com

Introducing the Value-Based BA Practice Framework

Value-based business analysis (BA) is emerging as a critical business practice for the 21st century. A successful business analysis practice working at the enterprise/strategic level of organizations is essential if we are to break the cycle of failed and challenged projects. It is a difficult and complicated endeavor to transition from tactical, project-based business analysis to enterprise/strategic business analysis, but one we must undertake. Here we introduce a framework that provides the roadmap to successfully implementing and sustaining value-based business analysis practices.

21st CENTURY CHALLENGES

These are tumultuous times. Businesses face unprecedented challenges in the hyperconnected 21st century global economy. Extraordinary gale-force winds of change are swirling faster than ever before, causing us to rethink our approach to business analysis and project management.

These challenges include the following:

- *Integrated economy.* Everyone is feeling the effects of the global integrated economy, and business analysts are no exception. Many jobs are becoming commoditized; they can be performed by contractors or outsourced to resources located anywhere across the globe. Global wage scales have made U.S. employees too expensive to perform standard, repetitive tasks. Many U.S. jobs are gone and are not coming back. Basic BA tasks are beginning to be outsourced or performed by contractors.

- *Technology and information explosion.* IT applications have also impacted U.S. jobs by automating repetitive activities, often increasing the quality and predictability of outcomes. Smart IT applications are replacing knowledge workers, including BAs, across many industries. The demand for new, innovative apps delivered quickly is making traditional requirements and development methods obsolete.

- *Convergence of digital, social, and mobile spheres.* Social/mobile media are connecting us all in obvious and subtle ways, some of which we don't yet fully understand, with new applications constantly emerging. As we have seen throughout the world, people are using social media to bring about major changes to social and political systems. BAs are using social media to enhance collaboration among key stakeholders across the globe.

- *Innovation vs. business as usual.* The call to action for today's businesses is "innovate or vanish." For businesses to be competitive, they must be first to market with innovative, leading-edge products and services that are intuitive and easy to use and that offer surprising new features. It is no longer enough for BAs to ask their business partners what they want or need. BAs must learn to foster creativity and innovation during their working sessions, continually asking the question: "Are we truly innovating?"

- *Business value realization.* Businesses cannot afford to waste project investments or precious resource time unless significant benefits in terms of innovation, value to the customer, and wealth to the bottom line will be realized. BAs understand the business value proposition and focus on value throughout the project. They work with project managers to develop release plans prioritized, based on business value, to deliver value early.

- *Project performance.* With business success riding on innovation and first-to-market speed, we must be able to deliver new products and business capabilities on time and within cost and scope commitments. However, according to the *CHAOS Manifesto 2013* by the Standish Group, technology-enabled business change initiatives are only 39 percent successful, as measured in terms of whether they are on time, on budget, and with the full scope of functions and features.[1]

This unrelenting change is compounded by unprecedented complexity at all levels—globally, nationally, locally, and within projects. With complexity comes dynamic, unpredictable, adaptive change. Projects are complex adaptive systems operating within a complex environment; thus, typical plan-based project and requirements management practices are insufficient when attempting to bring about speed and innovation. We find ourselves in a new, data-driven world where virtually all business projects are dependent on information technology (IT). And new technologies are complex by their very nature.

BREAKTHROUGH PRACTICES FOR THE 21st CENTURY

So what does all this have to do with business analysis?

There was a time in the not-too-distant past when no one understood what business analysts do. It was widely believed that inadequate requirements analysis work was a key cause of poor project performance and outright failure. It was also well understood that business analysis had to become more formalized: adopt new tools, techniques, methodologies, and structures to improve how BAs work. As a result, a progressive group of BAs in Canada gave birth to the International Institute of Business Analysis (IIBA), and business analysis transitioned from an informal *practice* to a rigorous *profession*.

IIBA provided us with these pioneering definitions:

On the art and science of business analysis—

Business analysis is the set of tasks and techniques used to work as a liaison among stakeholders in order to understand the structure, policies, and operations of an organization, and to recommend solutions that enable the organization to achieve its goals.

On the role of the business analyst—

Business analysts must analyze and synthesize information provided by a large number of people who interact with the business, such as customers, staff, IT professionals, and executives. The business analyst is responsible for eliciting the actual needs of stakeholders, not simply their expressed desires. In many cases, the business analyst will also work to facilitate communication between organizational units. In particular, business analysts often play a central role in aligning the needs of business units with the capabilities delivered by information technology, and may serve as a "translator" between those groups.[2]

In today's organizations, business analysts range from an entry-level role supporting small projects to a strategic role developing and implementing business transformation initiatives. Sometimes the role of the business analyst is viewed as a stepping stone toward becoming a project manager or business architect; however, we are seeing the growth of career paths for BAs from entry-level analysts to experienced enterprise/strategic BA consultants residing in the highest tiers or organizations.

EMERGING VIEW OF BUSINESS ANALYSIS

It's all about value—value to the customer and value to the bottom line of your organization. The business analysis profession is changing rapidly, adopting a more complete view of change initiatives. Today's BAs:

- Focus on delivery of business value and innovation vs. requirements management

- View change initiatives holistically, understanding the need to change people, processes, organizations, rules, data, applications, and technology

- Embrace architecture and design to help ensure project success

- Strike a balance between analysis and intuition, order and disruptive change.

Industry leaders across the globe are positioning business analysis as a critical business management discipline for the 21st century—and the cornerstone for their business transformation initiatives. BA's ultimate value proposition extends beyond tactical, project-aligned requirements management practices and encompasses delivering business solutions that:

- Add measurable business value

- Capitalize on complexity

- Innovate and differentiate business value

- Leverage technology for competitive advantage.

According to leading technology research firms, the business analyst is one of the hottest roles in business and in IT. Business analysis is the resource that is in high demand and will play a critical role in the future—not the junior role in IT or business functions that some BAs fill today.

The value-based role of business analysis creates vast new opportunities. Tomorrow's experienced and solution-focused BA professionals will add real value to their companies and foster innovation. These critical resources are already within your organization. Organizations that are able to harness the power of business analysis to drive value-creating change initiatives will be competitive in the 21st century.

BA PRACTICE IMPLEMENTATION AND SUSTAINABILITY FRAMEWORK

Implementing a more strategic BA practice is a formidable endeavor. Institutionalizing an enterprise-wide value-based BA practice is even more challenging. To enlist and sustain organizational support, the business value that BA practices promise needs to be fully understood across the organization, and BA benefits need to be continually demonstrated through measurement and communication programs. Leadership and sponsorship of the effort must emanate from the top and flow down to all levels of the organization. A holistic and methodical implementation approach and framework are essential for success and sustainability.

Mature BA practices have several well-oiled components: a capable BA team, organizational support, executive leadership and sponsorship, and an implementation and sustainability framework. Successful BA practices are supported by a number of integrated elements. To deal with the significant amount of change required by all stakeholders, the BA practice implementation should be managed in phases, following a disciplined framework (see Figure I-1).

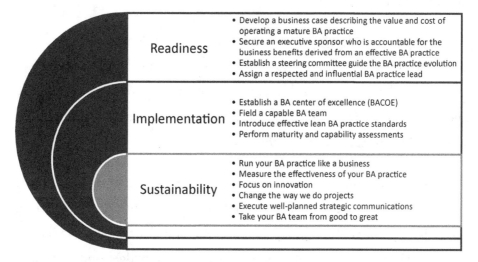

FIGURE I-1.   The Value-Based BA Practice Framework

A brief description of the elements of the framework is provided below, and each component is examined in detail in subsequent chapters.

THE INITIAL READINESS PHASE

The initial readiness phase answers the question, "Is our organization ready?"

Many elements must be in place for you to declare your readiness to begin to implement a BA practice. The most important tool for you to use to present your argument for a BA practice is the business case.

Unless your BA practice can demonstrate business benefits in terms of value to the customer and wealth to the bottom line, it will be a failed venture. Without a business case, you are likely steering a rudderless vessel. Developing the business case will enable you to think about all important aspects of the venture. Your BA practice business case must be convincing, compelling, and believable.

Once you have developed the business case to implement a BA practice, enlist an executive sponsor to guide the effort, to own the budget for the BA practice, and to commit to the cost and benefit projections. The executive sponsor is usually a senior-level executive, such as the chief information officer (CIO) or chief strategy officer (CSO).

It is ideal to secure the commitment of the experts who helped build the business case to serve on a BA practice steering committee. The steering committee, facilitated by the BA practice lead and chaired by the executive sponsor, will provide political cover, decision support, budget, and legitimacy to the BA practice initiative.

Building a new business process such as business analysis is a challenging endeavor. The BA practice lead is the person who is responsible for building the BA practice in an organization. This person may be a manager of BAs, but this is not always the case.

As the BA practice lead, your initial challenge is to gain executive confidence and organizational alignment up front. Do you have the power and influence skills to take a comprehensive view that is aligned with your organizational environment, culture, strategies, and decision-making practices?

THE SUBSEQUENT IMPLEMENTATION PHASE

The implementation phase answers the question, "How do we build the BA practice?"

The BA practice needs a home, a department that is accountable and responsible for building and sustaining effective BA practices. This center should be a manageable size and should be authorized to manage the BA team; the business case process; organizational BA standards and frameworks; methods, training, tools, templates, techniques, and metrics; and communication.

Today, BAs are mostly project-focused, creating and managing requirements artifacts. To become a valuable corporate asset, BAs need to become holistic thinkers who are strategically focused, concentrating on innovative solutions to complex business problems.

In days gone by, we followed the maxim, *process first, then tools.* The good news is that BA tools have grown up. Good BA standards are now embedded in integrated requirements management tools. So the tools help educate BAs on best practices, integrate and manage requirements knowledge and artifacts, and integrate engineering information into BA models and documents used to build the solution.

The bad news is that most BAs still use desktop tools that are difficult to maintain because they are not integrated. As a result, the BA is burdened with creating, maintaining, integrating, and synchronizing all of the business strategies, goals, models, documents, matrices, use cases, user stories, test cases, etc. You will need to adopt sophisticated tools to maintain reusable requirement artifacts, impose standards and consistency, and facilitate the education of your BA team.

Teams and organizations sometimes decline to conduct a maturity assessment because they know their capabilities are immature. The problem is, just knowing your capabilities are immature is not actionable. Assessments provide useful information about strengths to leverage and gaps that need immediate improvement to grow to the next level of maturity. Assessments shed light on exactly where you are, provide a step-by-step improvement roadmap, and target improvements based on proven maturity models.

It goes without saying that a 400-person organization with five business analysts will need much less process and structure than a 4,000-person global organization with 200 business analysts. When reviewing the individual elements of the value-based BA practice implementation framework, remember, less is more. Just enough is enough to move on. Don't fall into the trap of over-engineering your BA practice. Just as you scale the management and analysis of projects based on the needs of the effort, do the same when implementing your BA practice.

THE ONGOING SUSTAINABILITY PHASE

The ongoing sustainability phase answers the question, "How do we institutionalize and continue to improve our BA practices?"

Make no mistake: Implementing a mature BA practice is no small endeavor. The effort is fraught with challenges. Targeted measurements and effective communications tailored to the needs of each stakeholder group are essential to gain organizational support. The messages need to convey the real business value created by improved BA practices.

Continually increase the capabilities of your BA team and the maturity of your BA practice—and boast of your progress in every corner of your organization. Measure the business benefits of your BA practice and of projects in terms of value to your customers and wealth to the bottom line. Demonstrate value through performance measures that tie to your organization's corporate scorecard, project performance measures, and quality performance measures.

In this complex global economy, your organizational change initiatives need to result in innovative solutions; incremental changes to "business as usual" are no longer enough for organizations to remain competitive. Yet, many CEOs do not believe they have the creative leadership needed to capitalize on complexity to bring about innovation.

For BAs to reach their full potential and add the most value to their organizations, they must become creative leaders of innovative change. Traditional BA activities are still important, but a new focus on innovation is the 21st century call to action.

An organization's culture is durable because it is "the way we do things around here." Changing the way the organization selects projects, develops and manages requirements, and manages projects, while focusing not only on business value but also on innovation, likely represents a significant shift.

Use strategic communications as your most effective tool to ensure that you realize the full value of your BA practice. Recognizing that project sponsors seldom measure accurately and then communicate the value derived from project and program solutions, the BA practice lead ensures that these data are captured and shouted far and wide. To be taken seriously and to be looked upon as a credible leader of change, the BA practice lead must engage in strategic communications. This involves:

• Thinking strategically, holistically, and systematically

- Crafting powerful messages that are impactful and memorable

- Influencing positive decision-making through intentional and targeted strategic communication.

Complex projects are challenged today because of people failing to come together with a common vision, an understanding of complexity, and the right expertise. Virtually all work today is accomplished by teams of people, sometimes even *teams of teams* from around the globe. Team leadership is different from traditional management, and teams are different from operational work groups. When leading high-performing, creative teams, it is no longer about command and control; instead, it is about collaboration, consensus, empowerment, confidence, and leadership.

A View from on the Ground

THE CHALLENGE: TRANSFORMATION

Sandra Sears
IT Process & Practice Development
Insurance Industry

How does a successful traditional insurance company create an experience that meets the changing needs of customers and is competitive with new, non-traditional rivals? We chose to start by transforming the BA role from note taker to strategic partner. To maximize the likelihood of success, we brought in change consultants and practice experts. We even engaged an expert in cognitive sciences and intellectual capital management. We leveraged the teachings of change experts such as Dr. John Paul Kotter, author and American professor, who is currently the head of research at Kotter International and teaches in the High Potentials Leadership Program at the Harvard Business

School, and Kerry Patterson, a prolific writer who has co-authored numerous articles and award-winning training programs on innovation.

We learned that if we focused on outcomes we would fail; we needed to focus on behaviors— increasing our motivation to change and our ability to change. We realized that an organization can absorb only a certain level of change concurrently. We saw people suffer change fatigue. Initially, we heard many, many requests for process changes; as we evaluated and began to introduce changes and improvements, we heard "Stop! Too much change too fast."

PUTTING IT ALL TOGETHER

WHAT DOES THIS MEAN FOR THE BUSINESS ANALYST?

If you are working to implement BA best practices, methodologies, frameworks, and enabling technologies on your project, don't get discouraged. Collaborate with others outside of your project to expand your reach and build lasting momentum.

WHAT DOES THIS MEAN FOR THE BA MANAGER/PRACTICE LEAD?

Customize the framework to implement and sustain an enterprise-wide value-based BA practice that is strategically focused. Use it!

NOTES

1   The Standish Group, "CHAOS Manifesto, 2013: Think Big, Act Small," 2013. Online at versionone.com/assets/img/files/ChaosManifesto2013.pdf. (accessed January 2014).

2   International Institute of Business Analysis, *A Guide to the Business Analysis Body of Knowledge® (BABOK Guide®)*, 2009.

PART I
Readiness: It's All About the Culture

s your organization ready to support a new or advanced BA practice? We define readiness as having the following elements in place:

- A *business case* describing the value and cost of implementing a mature BA practice

- An *executive sponsor* who is accountable for the business benefits derived from an effective BA practice

- A *steering committee* to guide the BA practice evolution

- A respected and influential *BA practice lead.*

Chapter 1 addresses how you can assess the culture in your organization and the need to develop a strong business case for a new/advanced value-based BA practice. We present a proven approach to building the business case. In addition, we focus on establishing the governance infrastructure for your practice: an executive sponsor and a BA practice steering committee.

In Chapter 2, we explore whether you have an influential BA practice lead who is capable of implementing an effective value-based BA practice.

CHAPTER 1
Is Your Organization Ready?

I n this chapter we discuss the need for developing a business case to propose an enterprise-wide BA practice that is value-based and strategically focused. Do not be tempted to eliminate or truncate this important step. The business case development process will help you make the tough decisions and will enable you to customize the practice to your organization's needs. A business case will be your invaluable tool for proposing a breakthrough BA practice.

The Standish Group has been alerting us for decades that businesses are dependent on complex, technology-enabled business transformation projects for their success, yet we have been extremely challenged to perform projects satisfactorily. The focus has all too often been exclusively on requirements for IT solutions and then on managing (most often, limiting) changes to those requirements (generally regarded as scope creep).

The relatively new discipline of business analysis rethinks the change initiative context and shifts the focus from IT to the business, from technology to business value. BA shows us that business value should be at the heart of our efforts and that business benefits should drive our decisions. After all is said and done, it is about the business value that new solutions bring, not about the features and functions we think the technology should perform.

Despite the application of some world-class practices, far too many attempts to implement value-based BA practices have been only marginally successful. Too often the improvements to BA practices have been driven from the bottom up. While support is needed from all levels of the organization, grassroots efforts tend to be project-specific and therefore disappear gradually as project teams are disbanded.

It is through the business case for implementing a new, value-based BA practice that you can elicit high-level, top-down support. And it is through the effort you invest in building the business case that you will begin to gauge your organization's readiness to implement strategy-level BA practices.

ASSESSING THE CULTURE IN YOUR ORGANIZATION

Before you initiate the effort to build a business case for implementing a value-based BA practice, you will need to identify your organization's key issues and consider how business cases are used to drive change initiatives.

Projects are essential to the growth and survival of organizations today. Projects create value through capability-building business processes and through new products and services, responding to competition and changes in the marketplace. Make no mistake: Your effort to implement a value-based BA practice is a major project, and it will likely compete with other project ideas for resources and funding. Your organization is not going to support you simply because you think it is the right thing to do. The business case is your vehicle for eliciting support for investing in the effort.

In many organizations today, the business case is treated more as a formality than as a critical component of strategy execution and value creation. Far too many projects do not even have a business case. If there is one, it is typically created as quickly as possible and is used simply to secure resourcing and funding.

If your organization is currently not optimizing its use of business cases to help make strategic decisions about investments, this is your opportunity to model best practices for using the business case. The purpose of the business case is not only to secure funding, but also to drive value-based decision-making throughout all levels of the organization.

BUILDING THE BUSINESS CASE FOR THE BA PRACTICE

The life of every important change initiative should begin and end with a business case. Unless a change initiative results in value to the customer and wealth to the bottom line, it is a failed venture—even if it is delivered on time and on budget. The business case presents the expected costs and benefits of the proposed venture. Without it, you are steering a rudderless vessel. The BA practice manager/lead can demonstrate the value of business analysis through execution and management of the business case.

GATHER THE EXPERTS

Implementation of a new business process such as business analysis is a major cultural change effort. You will not get the organizational support you need unless you make a convincing case. During the readiness phase of the effort, engage a small but influential team of business and technology experts to work with you to build the business case for implementing a value-based BA practice. It is imperative that you not build the business case in isolation. Involving experts who are notable leaders in the organization is critical. By involving influential experts, you will be building your team of high-level supporters.

MAKE THE CASE

You need to lead the group of experts through a discovery period to examine the value of the new/advanced BA practice. Walking through the business case elements will provide a solid structure for your deliberations.

Building a business case is fundamentally a developmental, creative endeavor. The effort requires adequate time, a skilled facilitator (the BA practice manager/lead), a strategic focus, and creative expert resources. You need to drive the effort so that you will begin to enhance your credibility as the BA lead. You *own* the business case—you develop and maintain the business case in collaboration with the organization's business and technology thought leaders. You subsequently must defend and report against the cost and benefit projections contained in the business case. Be sure to capture the names and titles of the experts engaged to create the business case. They will lend credibility and authority to the proposal.

GET STARTED

The first step in building a solid business case is for the team of experts to arrive at consensus on the vision and purpose of the BA practice. The business case accomplishes the following:

- States the vision, mission, purpose, values, strategic goals, business objectives, and measures of success for the BA practice

- Outlines the expected total costs and quantifiable business benefits

- Describes the change management and communication approaches

- Presents the complexities, risks, and issues, and addresses how they will be managed

- Sets the course for how you will take the BA practice from good to great.

DETERMINE YOUR VISION

A sample vision is: *Business analysis practices are transformed into a value-based management tool, business analysts are viewed as respected consultants, technology is used as a competitive advantage to bring about innovation, and critical change initiatives produce the forecast business benefits as documented in the business case.*

DEFINE THE PURPOSE

A sample purpose is: *The purpose of a value-based BA practice is to enable our company to build a world-class business analysis practice that delivers real business value.*

DEFINE THE OBJECTIVES

The following are some sample objectives:

- Integrate the practices of business analysis with business architecture, business process, business rules and decisions, and business strategy and transformation to build and sustain an aligned organization that drives business transformation and innovation.

- Build the capabilities to optimize or transform our business practices and strategize a new business direction.

- Transition our IT-enabled business projects from a focus on technology to a focus on business value.

- Ensure that adequate enterprise/strategy analysis is conducted prior to building a business case for a proposed new project to ensure that the business need is understood and the optimal, innovative solution is proposed.

- Increase our capability to elicit, analyze, prioritize, specify, and validate business requirements.

- Validate the assumptions and forecasts made in the business case throughout the solution development phases to continuously confirm the case for investment in projects.

- Measure the business benefits of newly deployed business solutions.

- Ensure that business benefits are achieved and technology is used as a competitive advantage.

THE ANATOMY OF A BUSINESS CASE

The business case is the capstone document for the BA practice. It puts forward the rationale—the business need—for a value-based BA practice and describes how you will demonstrate results in business benefits. If you are unable to demonstrate results, your venture will be perceived as a failure.

Typically, a business case to create a value-based business analysis practice will include the following elements:

1. Executive Summary

2. Business Vision

    a. Core purpose

    b. Core values

    c. Envisioned future (10–30 year goal)

    d. Vivid description of what the business will look like

3. Strategic Goals

4. Yearly Objectives

    a. Year 1

    b. Year 2

    c. Year 3

5. Alignment to Corporate Strategies

6. Stakeholders

7. Opportunity Analysis

    a. Business problem

    b. Business opportunity

    c. Desired outcome

8. Capabilities

    a. Current capabilities

    b. Capability gaps

9. Solution Approach

    a. Year 1

    b. Year 2

    c. Year 3

10. The Journey from Good to Great

    a. Risk management

    b. Change management

    c. Communication management

11. Return on Investment

    a. Total costs

    b. Business benefits

Appendix A provides a sample of a value-based business case.

Innovation experts are advising us to use a short and concise presentation approach to propose the value-based BA practice in the context of the customer and the innovative product. Some suggest no more than seven slides (assuming you are using PowerPoint for your executive presentation). Build the presentation to include these critical elements:

1. Breakthrough Business Analysis: The Path to Value

    • Tactical BA practices defined

    • Strategic, value-based BA practices defined

    • How did we get here?

    • Who participated in the proposal?

2. Customers of the BA Practice: Who Will Benefit?

    • Stakeholder/customer list

    • Customer situation

    • Customer need

    • Customer problem/challenge

3. BA Practice Concept: Why Do We Need to Change?

    • Practice vision

- Practice goals and objectives
- Strategic alignment

4. Discriminator: Why Now?
   - Current solutions and competitors
   - Competitive positioning
   - If we don't do it, then....

5. Feasibility: What Will It Take?
   - Technical feasibility
   - Cultural feasibility
   - Process feasibility
   - Economic feasibility
   - Marketing feasibility
   - Project feasibility

6. Value: What Are the Benefits?
   - Value to our customers
   - Wealth to our bottom line

7. Decision
   - Further effort to implement and sustain the practice
   - Further effort to manage uncertainties, risks, and complexities

ESTABLISH THE BA PRACTICE GOVERNANCE STRUCTURE

Once you have developed the business case to implement your BA practice, the next step is to formally establish your governance process.

SECURE AN EXECUTIVE SPONSOR

First enlist an executive sponsor to guide the effort, to own the budget for the BA practice, and to commit to the cost and benefit projections. Usually, the executive sponsor is a senior-level executive, such as the CIO or CSO. The higher the sponsor is in the organization, the more prestigious your BA practice will be regarded. Ideally, the BA practice manager/lead should report directly to the sponsor.

ESTABLISH THE EXECUTIVE STEERING COMMITTEE

It is ideal to secure the experts who helped build the business case to serve on the BA practice steering committee. Facilitated by the BA practice lead and chaired by the executive sponsor, the steering committee will provide political cover, decision support, budget, and legitimacy to the BA practice. In smaller organizations, this may be an advisory group.

A View from on the Ground

ANALYST ADVISORY GROUP

Kate Gwynne
Associate Director, Business Analysis
Advertising Industry

Rather than the program management office (PMO) rolling out initiatives to the entire organization in a one-size-fits-all method, our PMO established an analyst advisory group to provide perspective, transparency, and clarity in implementing BA initiatives:

Perspective	Transparency	Clarity
Representation from several role types (BA, BSA, PM) across the departments within the organization	Communication and idea exchange throughout the design, development, and implementation process for each initiative	Content review and evaluation for fairness, accuracy, and relevance

MANAGE TO THE BUSINESS CASE

After assessing your influence and capabilities, you are ready to transition to implementation planning. Design the BA practice to meet the business need, scaled to the size of your organization, and ensure that you realize the benefits forecasted in the business case.

Typically, the business case is no longer used once the practice has been approved, resourced, and funded, and implementation is underway. However, as you elicit detailed business requirements and the value-based BA practice design emerges, continue to validate expected costs and benefits, updating the business case. Alert your executive sponsor and steering committee if the original assumptions or projections are at risk, and recommend a course correction. This validation/update cycle is essential to keep the business case alive and to keep everyone's focus on the business benefits. Remember, the business case is developed when we know the least about the endeavor, so it will lose its validity unless it is updated as more is learned.

After the BA practice is deployed, measure the value of the practice. If the value does not measure up to the original benefit projections, make adjustments and improvements. Manage so that the worth of the BA practice is directly related to value to the customer and benefits to the business, both of which lead directly to wealth to the bottom line.

FIRMLY ESTABLISH THE BA PRACTICE LEAD ROLE

Building a new business process such as strategic-level business analysis is a difficult endeavor that is riddled with obstacles. Your initial challenge is to gain executive confidence and organizational alignment. It is important to accomplish this up front. Do you have the power and influence skills to take a comprehensive view that is aligned with your environment, your culture, your strategies, and decision-making practices? Chapter 2 will help you assess whether you are ready.

As you make decisions and build the business case with your expert team, design compelling communication graphics for you all to use to begin to tell your story consistently.

PUTTING IT ALL TOGETHER

WHAT DOES THIS MEAN FOR THE BUSINESS ANALYST?

If you are working to implement BA best practices, methodologies, frameworks, and enabling technologies on your project, consider a wider implementation to other projects. This will help build momentum for a more value-based BA practice.

WHAT DOES THIS MEAN FOR THE BA MANAGER/PRACTICE LEAD?

This chapter argues for the need to develop a business case for a value-based, strategically focused BA practice implementation. Do not be tempted to eliminate or truncate this important step. The decision-making and risk review that will take place during the business case development will be invaluable to you going forward.

Now that you have assessed your organization's readiness to support a new or advanced BA practice, in Chapter 2 we explore whether you have an influential BA practice lead who is capable of implementing an effective value-based BA practice.

CHAPTER 2
Are You Ready to Be a Value-Based BA Practice Lead?

We have discussed the need for value-based business analysis practices as well as the need for a business case to implement new BA practices. In this chapter, we discuss how you as BA practice lead or BA manager and your senior BA team members can ensure that you are ready to lead the effort to implement and sustain the BA practice.

BE A POSITIVE POLITICIAN

Building a new business process such as business analysis is a challenging endeavor. First, you must gain executive sponsorship and organizational alignment. Do you have the power and influence skills to take a comprehensive view that is aligned with your organizational environment and decision-making practices?

Make no mistake: Organizational politics will influence your BA practice in multiple ways. Politics is really the collection of an organization's internal structures that deal with power, influence, and decision-making. Politics is often thought of in negative terms, but *positive politics* can lead to positive power and influence. Things happen when politics works. Decisions are made. Projects move forward. Deals are cut. Goals are met. Things get done. Your power is directly related to how well you negotiate the politics of your organization.

Your ability to act as a positive politician will have beneficial results for your team, for your organization, and ultimately for you. People want to follow natural leaders. You as BA practice manager/lead need to be seen as a leader.

As a positive politician, use your influence rather than authority or manipulation to achieve goals. Ensure that you are operating from a positive position—a solid basis from which to influence. This will include:

- *Status.* Your role as BA practice manager/lead needs to be positioned high enough in the organization to command respect.

- *Trust.* Your colleagues, whether on a peer level or above or below you on the organization chart, must trust you. Trust is earned slowly through positive interactions.

- *Integrity.* Never sacrifice your integrity. Never.

- *Consistency.* Maintain a "steady as she goes" posture. Carefully craft your communications so that they tell a story and are consistently positive and strategically oriented.

- *Knowledge.* Become a quick study. Know what you are talking about, and know when to dive into the details and when to stay at the executive level. Know your audience and what type of communication is appropriate to them.

CREATE YOUR POLITICAL MANAGEMENT PLAN

Devise strategies to negotiate your organization's politics by building your influence capabilities. Capture the strategies and tasks to achieve them in your personal political management plan (see Figure 2-1 for a sample). Strategies might include the following:

- Gain executive support, enlist the help of an executive sponsor

- Build partnerships, alliances, and coalitions

- Control critical resources

- Control the decision-making process

- Control your steering committee process

- Communicate strategically

- Manage cultural change

- Make yourself an expert, enhancing your credibility

- Promote yourself and business analysis

- Manage BA benefits

- Facilitate, negotiate, and build consensus

- Manage conflict.

Political Strategies	Gain Executive Support	Build Partnerships, Alliances, and Coalitions	Control Critical Resources	Control Decision Process	Control Steering Committee Process	Communicate Strategically	Manage Cultural Change
Strategy #1							
Actions							
Success Criteria							
Outcomes to Look For							
Validation Techniques to Use							
Strategy #2							
Actions							
Success Criteria							
Outcomes to Look For							
Validation Techniques to Use							

FIGURE 2-1. Sample Political Management Plan

BUILD AND MAINTAIN YOUR NETWORK OF SUPPORTERS

To build a positive network of supporters within your organization, identify your customers and the stakeholders who provide budget to your BA practice, provide oversight, provide requirements, provide input, get output, depend on your deliverables, and stand to benefit from your BA practice success. For each key customer/stakeholder, capture the following information:

- Role

- Awareness

- Opinion

- Importance

- Current level of support

- Level of support needed

- Issues and concerns regarding the BA practice
    - o What's in it for them?
    - o What do they need to view the BA practice positively and actively support it?

What actions can you take to increase the support of your most important stakeholders? What strategies will you devise to negotiate your organization's politics by building and sustaining a strong supportive stakeholder network? Capture the strategies and tasks to achieve the strategies in your political support network plan (see Figure 2-2 for a sample). Devise your strategies to lessen the impact of those who may negatively influence your BA practice and leverage those who are positive about you and business analysis.

Stakeholder	Role in Project	Awareness	Opinion	Importance	Support Needed	Existing Support	Influence Strategies
Stakeholder #1							
Stakeholder #2							
Stakeholder #3							

FIGURE 2-2.   Sample Political Support Network Plan

ASSESS THE ENVIRONMENTAL RISKS

Last, identify organizational and cultural risks to your success and devise strategies to manage those risks. Update your political management plan accordingly.

Assess the landscape:

- Environmental/organizational issues that are constantly at play

- Change the organization is undergoing

- Political games/maneuvers that are underway

- Power bases and power struggles

- Recent and anticipated leadership changes.

Assess how business analysis fits in:

- Is the business case for your BA practice solid? Does it describe the value and cost of implementing a value-based BA practice?

- Is implementation politically sensitive?

- Are there political implications?

- Will your core mission be impacted?

- Do you have a strong executive sponsor who is accountable for the business benefits derived from the BA practice?

- Do you have a strong executive steering committee that is passionate about implementing a value-based BA practice?

- What are the unspoken expectations?

- What is the decision-making process?

- What are the cultural norms?

- Is the communication and coordination effort challenging?

- Are you a respected and influential leader in your organization?

USE EXPERTS TO HELP

Some managers resent external consultants, thinking they come in, make obvious recommendations, and leave you to pick up the pieces. If you use internal or external experts, be sure they have been where you are going. Walk them through your political management plan so they understand your environment. Bring in experts to help accomplish the following:

- Assess organizational readiness and support

- Review your business case and plans

- Conduct a risk assessment

- Coach you through the process

- Gain approval and consensus on the way forward

- Form a guidance team/steering committee to involve upper management in the effort.

WHERE DOES THE BA PRACTICE LEAD RESIDE?

Positioning is equated with authority in organizational structures: The higher the placement, the more autonomy, authority, and responsibility are likely to be bestowed on the BA practice lead. Position the BA practice lead at the highest level possible to provide the measure of authority necessary to work across the organization while authenticating the value and importance business analysis has in the eyes of executive management. In the absence of high-level positioning, the BA practice lead's success and impact will likely be significantly diminished.

WHERE DOES THE BA TEAM RESIDE?

Another dilemma is whether the business analysts are centralized and report to the BA practice lead or are decentralized to be close to their customers. While there are pros and cons to both configurations, it is widely believed that a centralized BA team is needed to maintain a world-class BA practice.

- *Centralized BA team.* Having a centralized BA team that reports directly to the BA practice lead facilitates the implementation of new BA practices, makes development of a capable BA team with the skills needed by the organization easier, and makes quality assurance of BA deliverables much less complicated. However, the customers of the BA practice—the business units they serve—often feel less involved. They may feel less ownership in new business solutions because they believe the key decisions were made centrally rather than at their level. If you adopt this configuration, be sure to involve your customers closely in project decisions.

- *Decentralized BA resources.* Distributing BAs across the business and in IT allows them to be considered "part of the family." Decentralized BAs are closer to the customer and therefore often become credible experts about the business. They are likely trusted members of the business team, regarded as advocates for the business needs and priorities. On the other hand, it is much more challenging to implement standard practices, control BA career development, and ensure that business needs are met if BA resources are decentralized. In this structure, bring the BAs together often to foster team development, professional development, and consistency.

A View from on the Ground

ANALYST ADVISORY GROUP

Kate Gwynne
Associate Director, Business Analysis
Advertising Industry

Decentralization of BA resources usually means that the BA practice lead has responsibility for the success of BA-related initiatives without authority over the BAs. This model relies heavily on the practice lead's ability to persuade managers and executives to continue to support BA initiatives when other projects are vying for their resources.

The upside to the decentralized model is that BAs who report to individual departments are more in tune with departmental goals and have relationships with domain stakeholders—a huge advantage.

A possible compromise is a dotted-line reporting structure to both the practice lead and the business manager, so the BA has goals that relate to the BA practice but is focused on business-specific projects.

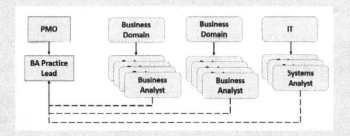

Another possibility is to route BAs through the PMO temporarily, so they can gain knowledge in best practices and management and analysis techniques, and then move them out to the business domains.

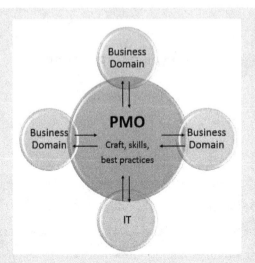

Both methods have merit and both require a strong practice lead and executive level support to implement.

Today's BA roles are typically decentralized, either IT- or business-oriented:

- *IT-oriented analysts* improve business results through changes to technology. These BAs are mostly generalists, with specialists emerging that may include experience analysts, business rules analysts, business process analysts, and data analysts.

- *Business-oriented analysts* improve operations through changes to policy and procedures. Business-oriented BAs are mostly specialized within a business domain, focused on finance, human resources, marketing, manufacturing, etc. In decentralized organizations, these analysts are dedicated to a major business area, improving the processes and the corresponding technologies that are used to run that operation. In more centralized organizations, these business analysts are organized as a pool of talent whose efforts can be transferred seamlessly to the areas of the enterprise that are most in need of business analysis support.

BA roles are expected to become more strategic, driving BA practice maturity to meet the 21st century needs of our organizations. These roles will likely be centralized, and they will likely include the business architect and the business/technology enterprise business analyst:

- *Business architects* strive to make the enterprise visible. They develop the business architecture—rich pictures and documentation that depict the current state of the business in terms of organizational structure, process and data flows, lines of business, locations, etc. They are also responsible for keeping the business and IT architectures in alignment. Business architects then create the future-state architecture to depict how the enterprise will look when the vision is realized and the strategy is executed. Only then can they identify the gap in capabilities that need to be filled to execute strategies.

- *Business/technology enterprise business analysts* are cross-domain experts who convert business opportunities into innovative business solutions, and translate strategy into breakthrough process and technology change. They keep their eyes on the competition and forge new strategies.

Whether business analysts are grouped together or are dispersed by time and distance, many companies have created business analysis centers of excellence (BACOE). A center of excellence provides a framework within which all business analysts in an organization conduct their work, usually consisting of processes, procedures, templates, tools, and best practices. In addition to providing guidelines and standards, a BACOE provides a forum for focusing on continuous improvement for the business analysis discipline. We will examine the BACOE in Chapter 3 when we discuss the organization structure supporting your BA practice.

PUTTING IT ALL TOGETHER

WHAT DOES THIS MEAN FOR THE BUSINESS ANALYST?

If you are trying to implement BA best practices, methodologies, frameworks, and enabling technologies on your project, the influence capabilities described in this chapter apply to you as well as to your BA practice lead. Work with the key leaders on your project to examine your collective power and influence as well as the landscape within which you are operating, and then develop a political management plan. In addition, start preparing yourself right now to meet your organization's needs.

WHAT DOES THIS MEAN FOR THE BA MANAGER/PRACTICE LEAD?

This chapter presents the case for a BA practice lead to examine political implications, including influence, power, support, and environmental issues. Diagnose your own political strengths and gaps. You need strong influence skills to get people to want to support your effort. Develop a political management plan to enhance your ability to negotiate organizational politics as well as your personal power and influence to achieve your goals. In addition, examine the optimal placement of business analysts in your organization.

We now turn to the next phase of establishing a world-class BA practice: implementation.

PART II
Implementation: It's All About the Fit

Once you have assessed your organization's and your own readiness to implement a new or advance an existing BA practice, you will be ready to turn your attention to: "How do we build the BA practice?" Implementation involves several key elements:

- A home for your BA practice

- A capable BA team

- Effective, lean BA practice standards.

A HOME FOR YOUR BA PRACTICE

In Chapter 3 we examine the types of models typically used to provide a "home" for the BA practice. The BA practice home is a department that is accountable and responsible for building and sustaining effective BA practices. The model most often used is a BA center of excellence (BACOE). This center should be small enough to be manageable and is typically authorized to manage the BA team, the business case process, organizational

BA standards and frameworks; methods, training, tools, templates, techniques, and metrics; and communication.

A CAPABLE BA TEAM

Today, BAs are mostly project-focused, creating and managing requirement artifacts. To become a valuable corporate asset, BAs need to become holistic thinkers who are strategically focused, concentrating on innovative solutions to complex business problems. In Chapter 4 we present a groundbreaking approach to building a capable BA team.

EFFECTIVE BA PRACTICE STANDARDS

Traditionally, we followed the maxim, *process first, then tools*. The good news is that BA tools have grown up. Good BA standards are now embedded in integrated requirements management tools. The tools help educate BAs on best practices, integrate and manage the requirements knowledge and artifacts, and integrate engineering information into the BA artifacts that are used to build the solution. The bad news is that most BAs still use desktop tools that are difficult to maintain and are not integrated. As a result, the BA is burdened with creating, maintaining, integrating, and synchronizing all of the business strategies, goals, models, documents, matrices, use cases, user stories, test cases, etc. In Chapter 5 we focus on the sophisticated tools that today's BAs need to adopt to maintain reusable requirement artifacts, impose standards, and enable the education of the BA team.

We also discuss the need for periodic maturity assessments in Chapter 5. It is often said that we don't need to do a maturity assessment because we know that our capabilities are immature. The problem is, just knowing that your capabilities are immature is not actionable. Assessments provide useful information about strengths as well as identify gaps that need immediate improvement to grow to the next level of maturity. Assessments shed light on exactly where you are, provide a step-by-step improvement roadmap, and facilitate continuous improvements based on proven maturity models.

CHAPTER 3

Establishing a Home for Your BA Practice

One of a BA practice manager/lead's key responsibilities is to examine the organization to determine the best fit for placement of the BA practice based on cultural, environmental, and maturation considerations. Perhaps a less formal structure is appropriate initially to build the foundation and credibility needed to implement a full-service, value-based BA center of excellence. Leverage your organization's structures and power bases to launch your BA practice, constantly demonstrating the value of business analysis.

A center of excellence is a team of people that is established to promote collaboration and the application of best practices. Centers of excellence are emerging as a vital strategic asset to serve as the primary vehicle for managing complex change initiatives. Within an organization, a center of excellence may refer to a small group of people, a department, or a shared facility. It may also be known as a competency center or a capability center. In technology companies, the formation of a center of excellence is often associated with new software tools, technologies, or associated business concepts such as service-oriented architecture or business intelligence.

THE BUSINESS ANALYSIS CENTER OF EXCELLENCE

The business analysis center of excellence (BACOE) is an emerging business practice—a new type of center that serves as the single point of accountability for everything that is business analysis. The BACOE defines the business architecture, rules, processes, data and knowledge, skills and competencies, and tools the organization uses to carry out business analysis activities throughout the project life cycle, from strategic planning to project initiation to solution delivery and benefits realization.

As the discipline of business analysis becomes professionalized, it is no surprise that BACOEs are emerging all around us. Staffed with knowledgeable business and technology experts, these centers are fulfilling a vital need in organizations today—providing a business-focused home for current business analysis practices, technologies, and emerging trends. The BACOE serves as an internal consultancy and information broker to both project teams and executive management. In addition, the BACOE is responsible for the improvement, and sometimes transformation, of business analysis practices. To that end, the BACOE continually evaluates the maturity of business analysis and implements improvements to overall business analysis capability. It is the BACOE that reports on the business benefits of project deliverables and of the BA practice itself.

It is a challenge, however, to establish a center of excellence that is accepted and supported by the organization. Considerable effort and due diligence are needed to make sure the new center is successful.

For a BACOE to be viewed as adding value, one of the critical functions it must perform is benefits management, a continuous process of identifying new opportunities, envisioning results, implementing, checking intermediate results, and dynamically adjusting the path leading from investments to business results. The role of the high-value BACOE is multidimensional, including: (1) providing thought leadership for all initiatives to confirm that the organization's investments are innovative solutions, (2) conducting feasibility studies and preparing business cases for proposed new projects, (3) participating in all strategic initiatives by providing expert business analysis resources, and (4) conducting benefits management to ensure that strategic change initiatives provide the expected value. The BACOE is staffed with credible business/technology experts who act as central points of contact to facilitate collaboration among the lines of business and the IT groups.

IMPLEMENTING THE BACOE

Once you have completed the readiness phase, your attention should turn to establishing a BACOE that is customized to fit your organization.

INTEGRATION

Although the BACOE is by definition business-focused, it is of paramount importance for successful centers to operate in an environment where business operations and IT are aligned and in sync. In addition, the disciplines of project management, solution design and development, and business analysis must be integrated. Therefore, to achieve a balanced perspective, it is important to involve business operations, IT, PMO representatives and project managers, and representatives from the portfolio governance group in the design of the BACOE. Indeed, your organization may already have one or more centers of excellence. If that is the case, consider combining them into one centralized center focused on program and project excellence. The goal is for a cross-functional team of experts (business visionary, technology expert, project manager, and business analyst) to address the full-solution life cycle from business case development to continuous improvement and support of the solution for all major projects.

BUSINESS DRIVERS

Understanding the business drivers behind establishing the BACOE is of principal importance. The motive for establishing the center must be unambiguous, since it will serve as the foundation for establishing the purpose, objectives, scope, and functions of the center. The idea to set up a BACOE might have originated in IT, because of the number of strategic, mission-critical IT projects impacting the whole organization, or in a particular business area that is experiencing a significant level of change. Whatever the genesis, strive to place the center so that it serves the entire enterprise, not just IT or a particular business area.

ORGANIZATIONAL PLACEMENT

One of the biggest challenges for the BACOE is to bridge the gap between business and IT. To do so, the BACOE must deliver multidimensional services to the many diverse groups. Regardless of whether there is one center of excellence or several more narrowly focused models, the BACOE organization should be centralized. Centralization fosters consistency and coordination, minimizing duplication of effort, confusion, and political maneuvers for control. It also enables organizations to configure and develop their IT systems by business process rather than by business unit, leading to more efficient and more streamlined systems operations. Whether large or small, best-in-class BACOEs evaluate the impact of proposed changes on all areas of the business and allocate resources and support services according to business priorities and business value.

Positioning is equated with authority in organizational structures; the higher the placement, the more autonomy, authority, and responsibility will likely be granted to the center. Therefore, position the center at the highest level possible in the organization.

ONE SIZE DOES NOT FIT ALL

To find the "perfect fit" for your BA practice center, take these elements into consideration, tying your vision, mission, and purpose to them:

- *Maturity of the organization's processes and capabilities.* The current state of the organization must be taken into consideration, including the effectiveness of strategic planning and project portfolio management practices, business performance management processes and strategies, business and technology architectures, development and support processes, and the strength of the business focus across the enterprise. Clearly, organizations with more mature practices achieve higher levels of value from their COEs.

- *Size of the organization and level of change.* Organizations can effectively absorb a limited amount of concurrent change, while maintaining productivity levels, at any given time. Therefore, a gradual approach to implementing the BA center is recommended. One option is to adopt a three-phased approach, moving across the BACOE maturity continuum from a project-focused structure to a strategic organizational model.

- *Size of your BA team.* How many BAs are enough? How many are too many? This depends on how many critical change initiatives are ongoing at any point in time. As software and other product development tools become more sophisticated, more BAs are needed to ensure a focus on business value. It is advisable to err on the small side; too big can be viewed as too costly.

- *Competitive pressure of the industry.* The higher the pressure to innovate products, services, and business capabilities and practices, the greater the need for the center.

BACOE MODELS

Several models of BACOEs are in use today (see Table 3-1). Each structure has a unique composition, goals, and outcomes. The type of center that is most appropriate depends on your organization's culture and politics. The center will be most effective when it has sufficient authority and influence. COEs run the gamut from purely advisory to enforcers of BA standard methods and tools. Often, the center plays an advisory role for some departments and a decision-making and enforcer role for others. If your organization already has centers of excellence in place, the BACOE concept will likely be more readily accepted. If not, you will need to tread lightly at first until you gain support and trust.

BACOE Model	Leader	Composition	Goals	Outcomes	Pros	Cons
1. BA community of practice	Senior BA	All BAs invited to participate	Serve as advisory resource center Raise awareness of the value of BA	Individual BAs begin to feel part of a professional team	Builds a BA community	No authority
2. Informal BACOE	BA team lead	Senior BAs	Establish basic BA standards Manage business requirements	Consistent BA deliverables and tools Business needs met	Builds the foundation for continuous improvement	Difficult to deploy and sustain standards without formal authority
3. Formal BACOE	BA practice lead Director/VP	All BAs report to BA practice director, either formally or dotted line	Conduct enterprise analysis and prepare business case Assign BA resources to projects Ensure quality and enforce standards Measure outcomes Execute strategy through projects and programs	Business value of project outcomes measured and communicated Strategy executed	Builds a professional BA practice BA considered a business consultant	Must demonstrate value or will be viewed as a cost
4. Integrated project/program management COE	Program management director/VP	BAs, PMs, and QA/testers report to COE director	Achieve 80% project success Improve competitive positioning Deliver value to customers and wealth to bottom line	Improved project performance Innovation New strategy forged	Builds a mature complex project management practice and value-based BA practice	Could result in too much power, process, bureaucracy

TABLE 3-1. BA Center of Excellence Models

As you begin to examine models for centers of excellence, you will find lots of variety. Most mid-to-large size organizations have multiple communities of practice. They may focus on different disciplines (e.g., project management, architecture, cloud computing) and may carry different names (e.g., IT process group, PMO). When you are considering the right fit for your organization, be certain to plug into the existing communities, especially if they are viewed as a positive force, so that processes will run smoothly end to end. This will help you gain instant credibility and acceptance as well.

The following "Views from the Ground" describe options that organizations have adopted for their BACOE.

A View from on the Ground

ANALYST COMMUNITY VS. CENTER OF EXCELLENCE

Kate Gwynne

Associate Director, Business Analysis

Advertising Industry

Here is one company's view of the differences between an informal community of practice and a formal center of excellence.

Analyst Community	Center of Excellence
Reporting structure: BAs dispersed among business/domain areas; report to managers who may/may not understand BA role	**Reporting structure:** Centralized BAs in PMO or other shared service department; report to practice lead(s)
Success relies on: BAs who are passionate about skills improvement and best practices; managers and executives who support BA practice within each domain; strong practice lead with ability to persuade, coach, mentor, and train	**Success relies on:** Executive support across organization; strong leadership with ability to manage, coach, and train BAs
Project staffing: BAs work on domain-specific projects, often regardless of expertise	**Project staffing:** BAs are assigned based on availability and expertise needed for project type
Role descriptions: May differ across the organization based on the actual job duties; more subject matter experts (SME) on business domains	**Role descriptions:** Consistent across organization; more in line with industry standards for skills and competencies
Career Path: Junior > Mid-level > Senior BAs; seniority and domain knowledge often override breadth and depth of analytical expertise	**Career path:** Junior > Mid-level > Senior > Strategic / Enterprise BAs; breadth and depth of analytical expertise overrides domain knowledge

A View from on the Ground

BUSINESS ANALYSIS COMMUNITY OF PRACTICE DEFINED

Sandra Sears

IT Process and Practice Development

Insurance Industry

The BA community of practice (BACoP) is a group of professionals working collaboratively to build the business analysis discipline. The mission of the BACoP is to evolve as the recognized source for enterprise business analysis collaboration, innovation, and knowledge sharing and to mature the BA practice in alignment with system development life cycle processes and industry standards.

A View from on the Ground

BUSINESS ANALYSIS COMMUNITY OF PRACTICE

Sandra Sears
IT Process and Practice Development
Insurance Industry

Here is a view of one company's multiple communities of practice with feedback links for integration.

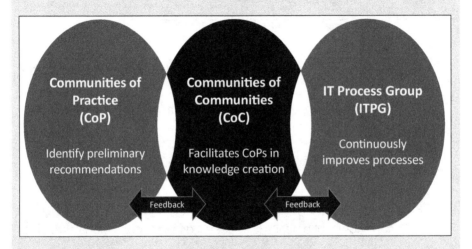

One of the key differentiators of these CoPs is that they have decision-making power. They vet all suggestions for process improvements within their discipline, prioritize them, and recommend them for action to the CoC, which assigns responsibility for design and implementation of the change. Design and implementation of the recommendation may be performed by the community itself or it may be handled by the IT process and practice development group.

A View from on the Ground

PMO-BA COMPETENCE CENTER

Michele Maritato

Project Manager, Business Analyst Consultant

In this organization several issues related to projects originated from the lack of competencies in business analysis and the lack of a consistent requirements management approach. The company decided to introduce the new role of "business analyst" and needed help developing and placing this role properly within the enterprise organization structure. Furthermore, the company wanted to develop a consistent requirements management approach across projects.

This company had an internal PMO that was managing and controlling all projects centrally; it made sense to create the new "business analysis competence center" within the PMO. In this way, BA competencies were centralized and the business analysts were placed at the same organizational level as project managers. The competence center was responsible for developing a consistent requirements management methodology across all projects.

THE FORMAL BACOE MODEL

If a formal BACOE is the best fit for your organization, we recommend a three-phased approach to implementation of a value-based BA practice center. In this approach, the center moves across the BACOE maturity continuum from a project-focused structure with limited influence to a strategic organizational model, and finally to a focus on innovation and the competitive positioning of the organization (see Figure 3-1).

FIGURE 3-1. BACOE Maturity Continuum

A truly comprehensive BACOE is broadly scoped and strategically placed to include the services, functions, tools, and metrics needed to ensure that the organization invests in the most valuable projects. The BACOE then delivers the expected business benefits from project outcomes in terms of value to the customer and wealth to the organization. A full-service BACOE typically performs the functions described in Figure 3-2.

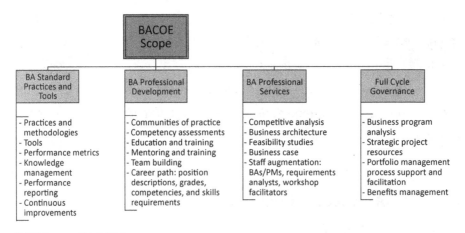

FIGURE 3-2. BACOE Scope

A fully functioning BACOE is capable of providing services across the spectrum of business analysis practices. The BACOE mission and objectives are met through training, consulting, and mentoring BAs and project team members; by providing BA resources to the project teams; by facilitating the portfolio management process; and by serving as the custodian of BA best practices.

WHERE TO START?

Based on the history of best practices for setting up centers of excellence, implementation involves four steps (see Figure 3-3):

1. Visioning and concept definition

2. Assessing the organizational knowledge, skills, maturity, and mastery of business analysis practices, and expectations of the BACOE

3. Establishing BACOE implementation plans

4. Finalizing plans and creating action teams to develop and implement the infrastructure to launch the center.

FIGURE 3-3. BA Centers of Excellence Implementation Approach

VISIONING

It is important to create a vision for the new center. This vision will be closely aligned with (or the same as) your vision for the BA practice that is included in the business case. Create a preliminary vision and mission/purpose statement for the center, developing the concept in enough detail to prepare a business case for establishing the center. Vet the proposal with key stakeholders and secure approval to conduct the assessment of business analysis practices and plan for the implementation of the center. The business case will likely be an update to or the same as the case prepared for the BA practice. Keep the business case alive, updating it as decisions are made and more is learned.

During meetings with key stakeholders, secure buy-in and support for the concept. Large-scale organizational change of this nature typically involves restructurings, cultural transformation, new technologies, and new partnerships.

ORGANIZATIONAL ASSESSMENT

The purpose of the organizational assessment is to determine organizational expectations for the BACOE and to gauge the cultural readiness for the center. Form a small assessment team to identify key challenges, gaps, and issues that should be addressed immediately. The ideal assessment approach is to conduct a formal organizational maturity assessment (discussed in detail in Chapter 5). However, a less formal assessment may suffice at this point. In addition, assess the current state of the following areas:

- BA acceptance by PMs, developers, architects, customers, managers, and other key stakeholders

- BA measures of success and incentives

- BA training and development programs

- BA formal or informal HR structures such as roles, career path, and pay scale (as compared to industry salary surveys).

This information will help you build your implementation and change management plans.

IMPLEMENTATION PLANNING

Develop a BACOE business plan and charter that describes the center in detail. Planning considerations include the elements listed in Table 3-2. It is helpful to draft the plan and charter, and then conduct a BACOE kickoff workshop where they are viewed, refined, and approved.

Agenda Items	Kick-off Workshop Agenda Items
Strategic Alignment, Vision, and Mission	Present the case for the BACOE, referencing the business case for more detailed information about cost versus benefits of the center.
Assessment Results	Include or reference the results of the assessments that were conducted: ° Organizational expectations of the BACOE ° Maturity of the business analysis practices ° Summary of the skill assessments ° Recommendations, including training and professional development of BAs and improvement of business analysis practice standards
Scope	Describe the scope of responsibilities of the BACOE, including: ° The professional disciplines guided by the center (e.g., PM and BA, just BA) ° The functions the center will perform ° The processes the center will standardize, monitor, and continuously improve ° The metrics that will be tracked to determine the success of the center

Agenda Items	Kick-off Workshop Agenda Items
Authority	Centers of excellence can be purely advisory or they can have the authority to own and direct business processes. The organizational placement should be commensurate with the center's authority and role. When describing the authority of the COE, include the governance structure (who or what group the COE will report to for guidance and approval of activities).
Services	A center of excellence is almost always a resource center, developing and maintaining information on best practices and lessons learned, and often assigns business analysts to projects. Document the proposed role: ° Materials to be provided (e.g., reference articles, templates, job aids, tools, procedures, methods, practices) ° Services to be performed (e.g., business case development, portfolio management team support, consulting, mentoring, standards development, quality reviews, workshop facilitators, providing business analysis resources to project teams)
Organization	Describe the BACOE team structure, management, and operations, including: ° Positions and their roles, responsibilities, and knowledge and skill requirements ° Reporting relationships ° Linkages to other organizational entities
Budget and Staffing Levels	At a high level, describe the proposed budget, including facilities, tools and technology, professional development, consulting services, and staffing ramp-up plans.
Implementation Approach	Document formation of initial working groups to begin to build the foundational elements of the center. In addition, describe the organizational placement of the center and its initial focus (i.e., project-centric, enterprise focus, or strategic focus).

TABLE 3-2.   BACOE Implementation Workshop Agenda

LAUNCHING THE BACOE

After the workshop session, finalize the BACOE charter and business plan, and launch the center. Form working groups to develop business analysis practice standards; provide for education, training, mentoring and consulting support; and secure the needed facilities, tools, and supplies.

A View from on the Ground

CHALLENGE: SUSTAINING THE TRANSFORMATION

Sandra Sears
IT Process and Practice Development
Insurance Industry

We adopted many strategies to ensure the changes were institutionalized and did not slowly erode. We established communities of practice and a community of communities, and made continuous improvement part of business as usual. We knew we needed a measurement and metrics program. We started simply, at first just letting data from metrics and feedback drive new, improved metrics. In addition, we discovered that we needed to learn and institutionalize the process before learning to use a new tool. Our management tool, PPM Central, was deployed more than a year after adoption of the processes.

PUTTING IT ALL TOGETHER

WHAT DOES THIS MEAN FOR THE BUSINESS ANALYST?

Today's BAs are performing their duties in a myriad of organizational environments. Determine where your organization is on the continuum and get involved in moving your BA practice to the next level by establishing or advancing a BACOE.

WHAT DOES THIS MEAN FOR THE BA MANAGER/PRACTICE LEAD?

The BA practice manager/lead should examine the organization to determine the best fit for the BACOE. Perhaps a less formal center of excellence is appropriate initially to build the foundation and credibility needed to implement a full-service, value-based BACOE. Leverage existing structures and power bases to launch your BACOE, constantly demonstrating the value of a mature BA practice.

Establishing centers of excellence is difficult because it destabilizes the sense of balance and power within the organization. Ambiguities arise when stakeholders are adjusting to the new model. These may manifest as resistance to change and can pose risks to a successful implementation. Therefore, coordinate and communicate about how the center will affect roles and responsibilities. Do not underestimate the challenges you will encounter from cultural resistance. Pay close attention to—and apply—organizational change management principles.

In Chapter 4 we present the case for a BA practice lead to build a capable BA workforce based on the complexity of current and future project assignments.

CHAPTER 4
Building Your BA Team

I t goes without saying that a successful BA practice requires a team of capable, credible business analysts. But being capable in BA practices is not enough in this complex, global world. As the complexity of projects increases, BAs need to be accomplished, perhaps gifted, strategic thinkers and leaders of change. Therefore, the first step in determining the optimal make-up of your BA team is to determine the type and complexity of work they are and will be performing. You will then be ready to take the next steps: determine the mix of BAs needed to build your capable BA workforce, and establish/refine your formal or informal BA career path.

STEP 1: ASSESS THE COMPLEXITY OF PROJECTS AND PROGRAMS

Before you begin to build your BA team, conduct an assessment of the current project portfolio and the backlog of potential projects for the next 12 to 18 months. The goal is to categorize projects according to their complexity. Using the Project Complexity Model 2.0 (see Tables 4-1 and 4-2), determine the profile of each project by selecting the cell that best describes the project for each complexity dimension, and then apply the formula following the model.

Complexity Dimensions		Project Profile			
		Level 1: Low Complexity Project	Level 2: Moderately Complex Project	Level 3: Highly Complex Project	Level 4: Highly Complex Program "Megaproject"
1. Size/Time/Cost		**Size:** 3–4 team members **Time:** < 3 months **Cost:** < $250K	**Size:** 5–10 team members **Time:** 3–6 months **Cost:** $250–$1M	**Size:** > 10 team members **Time:** 6–12 months **Cost:** > $1M	**Size:** Multiple diverse teams **Time:** Multi-year **Cost:** Multiple Millions
2. Team Composition and Past Performance		• **PM/BA:** competent, experienced • **Team:** internal; worked together in past • **Methodology:** defined, proven	• **PM/BA:** competent, inexperienced • **Team:** internal and external, worked together in past • **Methodology:** defined, unproven • **Contracts:** straightforward • **Contractor Past Performance:** good	• **PM/BA:** competent; poor/no experience with complex projects • **Team:** internal and external, have not worked together in past • **Methodology:** somewhat defined, diverse • **Contracts:** complex • **Contractor Past Performance:** unknown	• **PM/BA:** competent, poor/no experience with megaprojects • **Team:** complex structure of varying competencies and performance records (e.g., contractor, virtual, culturally diverse, outsourced teams) • **Methodology:** undefined, diverse • **Contracts:** highly complex • **Contractor Past Performance:** poor

Complexity Dimensions	Project Profile			
	Level 1: Low Complexity Project	**Level 2: Moderately Complex Project**	**Level 3: Highly Complex Project**	**Level 4: Highly Complex Program "Megaproject"**
3. Urgency and Flexibility of Cost, Time, and Scope	• **Scope**: minimized • **Milestones**: small • **Schedule/Budget**: flexible	• **Scope**: achievable • **Milestones**: achievable • **Schedule/Budget**: minor variations	• **Scope**: over-ambitious • **Milestones**: over-ambitious, firm • **Schedule/Budget**: inflexible	• **Scope**: aggressive • **Milestones**: aggressive, urgent • **Schedule/Budget**: aggressive
4. Clarity of Problem, Opportunity, Solution	• **Objectives**: defined and clear • **Opportunity/Solution**: easily understood	• **Objectives**: defined, unclear • **Opportunity/Solution**: partially understood	• **Objectives**: defined, ambiguous • **Opportunity/Solution**: ambiguous	• **Objectives**: undefined, uncertain • **Opportunity/Solution**: undefined, ground-breaking, unprecedented
5. Requirements Volatility and Risk	• **Customer Support**: strong • **Requirements**: understood, straightforward, stable • **Functionality**: straightforward	• **Customer Support**: adequate • **Requirements**: understood, unstable • **Functionality**: moderately complex	• **Customer Support**: unknown • **Requirements**: poorly understood, volatile • **Functionality**: highly complex	• **Customer Support**: inadequate • **Requirements**: uncertain, evolving • **Functionality**: many complex "functions of functions"

Complexity Dimensions	Project Profile			
	Level 1: Low Complexity Project	Level 2: Moderately Complex Project	Level 3: Highly Complex Project	Level 4: Highly Complex Program "Megaproject"
6. Strategic Importance, Political Implications, Stakeholders	• **Executive Support:** strong • **Political Implications:** none • **Communications:** straightforward • **Stakeholder Management:** straightforward	• **Executive Support:** adequate • **Political Implications:** minor • **Communications:** challenging • **Stakeholder Management:** 2–3 stakeholder groups	• **Executive Support:** inadequate • **Political Implications:** major, impacts core mission • **Communications:** complex • **Stakeholder Management:** multiple stakeholder groups with conflicting expectations; visible at high levels of the organization	• **Executive Support:** unknown • **Political Implications:** impacts core mission of multiple programs, organizations, states, countries; success critical for competitive or physical survival • **Communications:** arduous • **Stakeholder Management:** multiple organizations, states, countries, regulatory groups; visible at high internal and external levels

Complexity Dimensions	Project Profile			
	Level 1: Low Complexity Project	Level 2: Moderately Complex Project	Level 3: Highly Complex Project	Level 4: Highly Complex Program "Megaproject"
7. Level of Change	• **Organizational Change:** impacts a single business unit, one familiar business process, and one IT system • **Commercial Change:** no changes to existing commercial practices	• **Organizational Change:** impacts 2–3 familiar business units, processes, and IT systems • **Commercial Change:** enhancements to existing commercial practices	• **Organizational Change:** impacts the enterprise, spans functional groups or agencies; shifts or transforms many business processes and IT systems • **Commercial Change:** new commercial and cultural practices	• **Organizational Change:** impacts multiple organizations, states, countries; transformative new venture • **Commercial Change:** ground-breaking commercial and cultural practices
8. Risks, Dependencies, and External Constraints	• **Risk Level:** low • **External Constraints:** no external influences • **Integration:** no integration issues • **Potential Damages:** no punitive exposure	• **Risk Level:** moderate • **External Constraints:** some external factors • **Integration:** challenging integration effort • **Potential Damages:** acceptable exposure	• **Risk Level:** high • **External Constraints:** key objectives depend on external factors • **Integration:** significant integration required • **Potential Damages:** significant exposure	• **Risk Level:** very high • **External Constraints:** project success depends largely on multiple external organizations, states, countries, regulators • **Integration:** unprecedented integration effort • **Potential Damages:** unacceptable exposure

Complexity Dimensions	Project Profile			
	Level 1: Low Complexity Project	Level 2: Moderately Complex Project	Level 3: Highly Complex Project	Level 4: Highly Complex Program "Megaproject"
9. Level of IT Complexity	• **Technology:** technology is proven and well-understood • **IT Complexity:** application development and legacy integration easily understood	• **Technology:** technology is proven but new to the organization • **IT Complexity:** application development and legacy integration largely understood	• **Technology:** technology is likely to be immature, unproven, complex, and provided by outside vendors • **IT Complexity:** application development and legacy integration poorly understood	• **Technology:** technology requires ground-breaking innovation and unprecedented engineering accomplishments • **IT Complexity:** multiple "systems of systems" to be developed and integrated

TABLE 4-1. Project Complexity Model 2.0

Adapted with permission from *Managing Complex Projects: A New Model* by Kathleen B. Hass. © 2009 by Management Concepts, Inc. All rights reserved.

PROJECT COMPLEXITY FORMULA

Highly Complex Program "Megaproject"	Highly Complex Project	Moderately Complex	Independent
Size: Multiple diverse teams **Time:** Multi-year **Cost:** Multiple Millions *or* 2 or more in the **Highly Complex Program/Megaproject** column	**Organizational Change:** impacts the enterprise, spans functional groups or agencies, shifts or transforms many business processes and IT systems *or* Three or more categories in the **Highly Complex Project** column And No more than one category in the **Highly Complex Program/Megaproject** column	Three or more categories in the **Moderately Complex Project** column *or* No more than two categories in the **Highly Complex Project** column and	No more than two categories in the **Moderately Complex Project** column *and* No categories in the **Highly Complex Project** or the **Highly Complex Program/Megaproject** column

TABLE 4-2. Project Complexity Model 2.0 Formula

Adapted with permission from *Managing Complex Projects: A New Model* by Kathleen B. Hass. © 2009 by Management Concepts, Inc.

STEP 2: DETERMINE THE MIX OF BAs NEEDED TO BUILD YOUR CAPABLE BA WORKFORCE

Clearly, the skills required by both PMs and BAs differ widely depending on the complexity profile of their project assignments. Referring to the BA Individual/Workforce Capability Model (Table 4-3 and Figure 4-1), assess your needs by determining the number of BAs required at each level of complexity to execute current and anticipated projects. With this information, you are ready to begin to build your BA team staffing plan. The model is four-tiered for both project managers and business analysts and is consistent with the project complexity model. The levels of the model are based on the escalating complexity of typical project assignments.

Level	Area of Focus	Complexity Profile	Business Outcomes
1.	**Operations and Support Projects**	Low Complexity	Business operations are maintained and enhanced.
2.	**Project-Focused Projects**	Moderately Complex	Business objectives are met through projects.
3.	**Enterprise Projects**	Highly Complex Projects	Business strategy is executive through projects, programs, and portfolios.
4.	**Competitive Projects**	Highly Complex Programs	New business strategy is forged and competitive advantage is improved through innovation and business/technology optimization.

TABLE 4-3. BA Workforce Capability Model Matrix

LEVEL 1: OPERATIONS AND SUPPORT FOCUS

To maintain and enhance business operations, both generalists and system specialists are needed. These BAs typically spend about 30 percent of their time doing business analysis activities for low-complexity projects designed to maintain and continually improve business processes and technology. In the remaining time they are often fulfilling multiple roles, including developer, engineer, subject matter expert (SME), domain expert, and tester. As legacy processes and systems age, these BAs are becoming more valuable because they are likely the best (and often the only) SMEs who understand the current business processes and supporting technology. Many organizations are creating separate groups of PMs, BAs, and developers to manage maintenance of current business processes, the legacy systems that support them, and the vendors that help support the legacy IT operations.

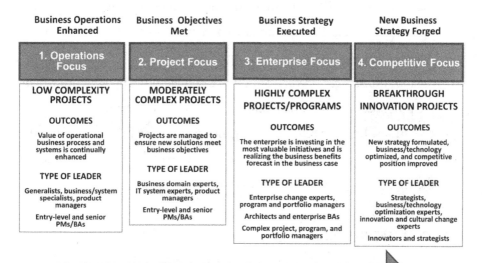

FIGURE 4-1. PM/BA Workforce Capability Model

LEVEL 2: PROJECT FOCUS

To ensure that business objectives are met through projects, both IT- and business-oriented BAs are needed. These BAs work on moderately complex projects designed to develop new/improved business processes and IT systems.

- *IT-oriented BAs* improve operations through changes to technology. These BAs are mostly generalists, with specialists that include experience analysts, business rules analysts, business process analysts, and data analysts.

- *Business-oriented BAs* improve operations through changes to policy and procedures. These BAs are usually specialized, focused on areas such as finance, human resources, marketing, and manufacturing. In decentralized organizations, these BAs are dedicated to a major business area, improving the processes and the corresponding technologies that are used to run the operations. In more centralized organizations, these BAs are organized as a pool of talent whose efforts can be transferred seamlessly to the areas of the enterprise that are in most need of project support.

LEVEL 3: ENTERPRISE FOCUS

This group includes seasoned PMs and BAs. The PMs are trained and experienced in managing highly complex projects, programs, and portfolios. The BAs often specialize into two groups: enterprise analysts and business architects. Both groups operate at the strategic level of the organization to ensure that BA activities are dedicated to the most valuable initiatives and that BA assets (deliverables/artifacts such as models and diagrams) are considered corporate assets and are therefore reusable. Enterprise PMs and BAs focus on the analysis needed to prepare a solid business case to propose new initiatives and work on highly complex, enterprise-wide projects; business architects make the enterprise visible and keep the business and IT architectures in sync.

LEVEL 4: COMPETITIVE FOCUS

Business/technology optimization BAs are business and technology visionaries who serve as innovation experts, organizational change specialists, and cross-domain experts. Business/technology BAs focus outside of the enterprise on what the industry is doing and design innovative new approaches to doing business to ensure that the enterprise remains competitive, or even leaps ahead of the competition. Business/technology BAs forge new strategies, translate strategy into breakthrough process and technology, and convert business opportunities into innovative business solutions.

The capabilities needed at each level of the model differ significantly. BA technical capabilities are needed at every level; leadership and soft skill competencies and techniques are needed to succeed on higher level, more complex projects. See Tables 4-4 and 4-5 for a listing of capabilities and techniques needed to perform successfully at each level of the model.

BA Technical Competency Areas
Level 1 and 2: Project-Focused
• *Business Analysis Planning and Monitoring
• *Elicitation
• ˣRequirements Management and Communication
• *Requirements Analysis
• Business Need
• Business Domain Scope Definition
• Requirements Specification and Documentation
• Requirements Validation
• System Maintenance and Enhancement

Level 3: Enterprise-Focused

- *Enterprise Analysis
- *Solution Assessment and Validation
- Business Case Development and Management
- Strategy Execution
- Organizational Change Management

Level 4: Competitive-Focused

- R & D
- Strategy Formation
- Creativity and Innovation
- Competitive Analysis
- Breakthrough Process and Product Design
- Cultural Change Management

Level 1 BA Techniques	Level 2 BA Techniques
Acceptance and Evaluation Criteria Definition	Baselining
Brainstorming	Business Case Development and Validation
Checklists	Business Process Analysis and Management
Continuous Process Improvement	Business Rules Analysis and Management
Defect and Issue Reporting	Change Management
Document Analysis	Conflict and Issue Management
Estimation	Consensus Mapping
Functional Decomposition	Communications Requirements Analysis
Interface Analysis	Business Process Design
Interviews	Data Dictionary and Glossary
Non-Functional Requirements Analysis	Data Flow Diagrams
Observation	Data Modeling
Problem Tracking	Decision Analysis
Replanning	Delphi
Requirements Change Management	Expert Judgment
Requirements Documentation	Focus Groups
Requirements Prioritization	Force Field Analysis
Sequence Diagramming	MoSCoW Analysis
Stakeholder Analysis/Mapping	Process Modeling
Time Boxing / Budgeting	Prototyping
Voting	

	Requirements Attribute Assignment
	Requirements Briefings and Presentations
	Requirements for Vendor Selection
	Requirements Traceability/Coverage Matrix
	Requirements Decomposition
	Requirements Workshops
	Requirements Review, Validation, and Signoff
	Responsibility Matrix (RACI)
	Reverse Engineering
	RFI, RFQ, RFP
	Risk Analysis
	Root Cause Analysis
	Scenarios and Use Cases
	Scope Modeling
	Sequence Diagrams
	Solution Modeling
	State Diagrams
	Structured Walkthroughs
	Survey/Questionnaire
	User Acceptance Testing
	User Stories and Storyboards
	Value Analysis
	Variance Analysis
	Vendor Assessment
Level 3 BA Techniques	**Level 4 BA Techniques**
Balanced Scorecard	Breakthrough Thinking
Benchmarking	Breakthrough Process Design
Business Architecture	Cultural Change
Business Case Development and Validation	Divergent Thinking
Business Opportunity Analysis	Edge-of-Chaos Analysis
Business Problem Analysis	Emotional Intelligence
Business Process Reengineering	Experimentation
Competitive Analysis	Idea Generation and Mind Mapping
	Innovation and Creativity

Cost/Benefit Analysis and Economic Modeling	Innovation Teams
Current State Analysis	Intuition
Feasibility Analysis	Investigation and Experimentation
Future State Analysis	Metaphors and Storytelling
Goal Decomposition	Mind Mapping
Gap Analysis	Pattern Discovery
Last Responsible Moment Decision-Making	Research and Development
Lessons Learned Process	Strategic Planning
Metrics and Key Performance Indicators	Systematic Inventive Thinking
Organizational Modeling	Visualization
Organizational Change	
Portfolio Analysis	
Project and Program Prioritization	
Root Cause Analysis (Fishbone Diagram)	
SWOT Analysis	

TABLE 4-4. BA Workforce Technical Competencies and Techniques by Level

*Source: International Institute of Business Analysis, *A Guide to the Business Analysis Body of Knowledge® (BABOK Guide®)*, 2009.

BA WORKFORCE SUPPORTING COMPETENCIES

Because both the project manager and the business analyst fill a leadership position in their organizations, driving change and improvements, they both need to possess effective knowledge, skills, attitudes, and behaviors that are related to successfully bringing about positive change through their projects (see Table 4-5). Supporting leadership competencies are also vital. BAs should begin to build these competencies early in their careers as they grow in experience and competence.

BA Supporting Competencies			
Analytical and Systems Thinking	**Business Knowledge**	**Personal Competencies**	**Interpersonal Skills**
• Decision-Making • Problem Solving • Systems Thinking • Creativity • Visioning • Innovation	• Business Principles and Practices • Industry Knowledge • Organizational Knowledge • Solution Knowledge • Software Application Knowledge	• Communicating • Leading • Managing • Cognitive Ability • Effectiveness • Professionalism	• Oral Communication • Written Communication • Teaching and Mentoring • Facilitation and Negotiation • Leadership • Influencing • Team Building

TABLE 4-5. BA Workforce Supporting Competencies

BUILD YOUR CAPABLE BA WORKFORCE FOR LEVELS 1 AND 2: LOW TO MODERATELY COMPLEX PROJECTS

There are likely many kinds of analysts within your business. Which of these are actually performing business analysis tasks? How do you cull through the various analysts in your organization to build your BA team? Because business analysts operate in both the business and IT worlds, they will arrive to your team from various fields. Some come from programmer/analyst positions, while others have conventional business expertise supplemented by IT prowess.

Take an inventory of the individuals currently serving in a requirements management role on your projects. Most will likely be operating at the first two levels of the model, focusing on requirements discovery and definition. This has long been considered the core business analysis function. These BAs should be defining, analyzing, and documenting requirements in a creative and iterative process to show *what* the new/changed business system will do and to explore options for *how* it will be done. Their requirements, in their textual and graphical form, should represent a depiction of the system. The requirements management process is typically subdivided into these activities: business need identification, scope definition, elicitation, analysis, specification, documentation, validation, management, and maintenance and enhancements.

Don't fall into the trap of believing that expertise in the IT components of the solution (solution designers and developers) is a key requirement for your business analysts. If you do, business analysis is likely to be treated as a subset of IT disciplines rather than as its own vital discipline. Time and again, projects encounter difficulties not from lack of IT expertise, but from an inability to keep the focus on the business, which is the most important role of the BA. When the focus is on IT, projects are often initiated, and design and construction of the IT solution is underway, before the development team members have a clear understanding of the business need or the most innovative solution. Often, tolerance is low for inadequate and ever-evolving requirements. Your job is to inspire your BAs to bring the focus back to the business need and business value.

When looking for candidates, both in the business areas and in IT, seek those who understand that business requirements analysis differs from traditional information systems analysis because of its focus, which is exclusively *adding value to the business*. Build a level 1 and a level 2 BA team that are capable of focusing on providing business objectives; business needs analysis; clear, structured, useable requirements; trade-off analysis; solution feasibility and risk analysis; and cost-benefit analysis. Assess the capabilities of the BAs you recruit, identify gaps, and create and execute a learning and development plan to close those gaps for your level 1 and 2 BAs. If needed, solicit the help of experienced BA consultants to ensure project success. Your goal is to significantly impact current projects in a positive manner.

A View from on the Ground

GREAT BUSINESS ANALYSTS

Kate Gwynne

Associate Director, Business Analysis

Advertising Industry

I've worked with and hired analysts who are knowledgeable BAs—well versed in requirements tasks, techniques, and deliverables. These folks are good analysts. But when building a BA practice, the BAs I find the most valuable and the best partners are BAs who are also expert communicators, collaborators, and facilitators. These people are walking billboards for the value BA provides. They naturally help improve project communication, reduce conflict and churn on projects, and are not shy about jumping in when they can provide value. These are *great* BAs, and it's exciting to set them loose on projects and watch people become believers in BA.

BUILD YOUR STRATEGIC BA WORKFORCE FOR LEVELS 3 AND 4: HIGHLY COMPLEX PROGRAMS AND PROJECTS

It is becoming increasingly clear that while level 1 and 2 BA competencies are necessary, they are insufficient for successfully managing requirements and arriving at the most innovative solution on the large, enterprise-wide, complex, critical projects that are the norm today. Just as a business leader must be multi-skilled and strategically focused, business analysts operating at the strategic level must possess an extensive array of leadership skills. As your BA practice matures, recruit systems-thinking BAs capable of assuming a leadership role on critical projects, and quickly elevate them to senior positions within the team. As the IT contribution moves beyond efficiency to business success, the business analyst becomes the central figure on the project team who must be "bilingual"—speaking both business and technical languages. To perform in this pivotal role, the business analyst must possess a broad range of knowledge and skills.

Individuals performing business analysis activities at the strategic level do not always consider themselves part of the BA career family. But make no mistake: This is the path for the talented and ambitious business analyst that leads to business architect and enterprise/strategic analyst. Look for individuals who have leadership qualities, are well respected, and carry influence within your organization to fill these most important BA roles.

While the business analyst is fast becoming a relatively senior position in the business world, historically it has been considered a mid- to low-level role. You need to work to change the perception of the BA as a requirements documenter to the BA as a valuable strategic consultant. A recent survey revealed an increasing demand for senior individuals who can perform the ever-widening range of strategic business analysis functions. Just like any leadership position, mastery of a unique combination of technical, analytical, business, and leadership skills is required (see Table 4-6).

Technical	Analysis	Business	Leadership
Systems engineering concepts and principles	Fundamentals of business operations	Business process improvement and reengineering	Project, program, and portfolio management
Complex modeling techniques	Ability to conceptualize and think creatively	Strategic and business planning; business architecture	Capacity to articulate vision; systems/holistic thinking
Communication of technical concepts to non-technical audiences	Techniques to plan, document, analyze, trace, and manage requirements	Communication of business concepts to technical audiences	Organizational change management; management of power and politics
Testing, verification, and validation	Requirements risk assessment and management	Business outcome thinking	Problem solving, negotiation, and decision-making
Technical writing	Administrative, analytical, and reporting skills	Business writing	Team management, leadership, mentoring, and facilitation
Rapid prototyping	Cost/benefit analysis	Business case development	Authenticity, ethics, and integrity
Technical domain knowledge	Time management and personal organization	Business domain knowledge	Customer relationship management

TABLE 4-6. Technical, Analytical, Business, and Leadership Skills

STEP 3: ESTABLISH/REFINE YOUR FORMAL OR INFORMAL BA CAREER PATH

For business analysis to be considered a key position in your organization, it must have a clear career path. The trend today is to map the business analyst role from entry to senior levels of organizations.

THE REAL BUSINESS ANALYST: ROLE OR TITLE?

Many job titles are used for individuals performing BA activities, including business analyst, business systems analyst, business system planner, business architect, business rules analyst, and even principal solutions architect. Regardless of the job title, a strong, experienced business analyst is critical to complex project success. Depending on the level of responsibility and placement in the organization, business analyst duties at all levels include the following:

- Identify and understand the business problem and the impact of the proposed solution on the organization's operations

- Document the complex areas of project scope, objectives, added value, and benefit expectations, using an integrated set of analysis and modeling techniques

- Translate business objectives into system requirements using powerful modeling tools

- Assist in determining the strategic direction of the organization by evaluating customer needs, thus contributing to the strategic planning of transformational change and technology directions

- Liaise with major customers during preliminary installation and testing of new products and services

- Design and develop high-quality, innovative business solutions.

THE BUSINESS ANALYST CAREER ROAD MAP ACCORDING TO IIBA

The International Institute of Business Analysis provides sound guidance to help organization create a career path for BAs. According to Maureen

McVey, CBAP, Head of Learning Development for IIBA, the IIBA Career Road Map depicts "business analysis opportunities for those wishing to enter this growing profession. It also provides direction for business analysts looking for senior positions, and includes the emerging roles in business architecture and business intelligence, roles which are in high demand."

McVey explains that "your BA career is a journey, with many entry and exit points." McVey suggests that the BA practice lead work with each BA to identify his or her current position from the many role families, and determine aspirations for future roles. These role families include the following:

- Business-Focused
    - o Business requirements analyst
    - o Business process analyst
    - o Decision analyst (often referred to as a business intelligence analyst)

- IT Analyst
    - o Business systems analyst
    - o Systems analyst
    - o Functional analyst
    - o Service request analyst
    - o Agile analyst

- BA Leadership
    - o BA project lead
    - o BA program lead
    - o BA practice lead
    - o Relationship manager
    - o BA manager

- Enterprise Level
    - o Enterprise architect
    - o Business architect.

McVey goes on to say: "Director, Vice President, even C level positions are on the BA path! The business analyst is the perfect candidate!"[1]

PUTTING IT ALL TOGETHER

WHAT DOES THIS MEAN FOR THE BUSINESS ANALYST?

If you are a practicing BA, determine the complexity of your current project assignments and identify gaps in the capabilities you need to be successful. If you have significant gaps in BA capabilities, work with the project manager and your BA practice manager/lead to fill those gaps. In addition, identify the level of BA work to which you aspire, and draft your personal learning and development plan to achieve the level of your choice.

WHAT DOES THIS MEAN FOR THE BA MANAGER/PRACTICE LEAD?

This chapter presents the case for a BA practice lead to build a capable BA workforce based on the complexity of project assignments. Use these tools and this approach to BA team recruiting and development to build your world-class, value-based BA practice. Update your implementation plans for the BACOE with a staffing plan to document the results of your needs assessment and the activities you have identified to build a capable BA team.

Remember, you cannot rely on recruitment alone. You must develop current BAs as well through programs for high-potential employees, succession planning, training, coaching, and mentoring. Look for passionate BAs who share your vision and values.

In Chapter 5 we present the critical steps to determine the current state of your BA practices and to build a roadmap to increase the maturity of your methods and tools.

NOTES

1   McVey, Maureen, "The Business Analyst Career Road Map according to IIBA," February 2014. Online at *www.iiba.org/ba-connect/2013/june/business-analyst-career-roadmap.aspx* (accessed February 2014).

Determining the Current State of Your BA Practices and Closing the Gaps

A long with a team of capable, credible business analysts and a well-placed and influential BACOE, a successful BA practice requires effective, lean methods and tools. Use the experience and talent of your BA team to assess, develop, and improve BA practices. Focus on all aspects of your practices, including people, process, and tools.

In this chapter we present the critical steps to determine the current state of your BA practices and to build a roadmap to increase the maturity of your methods and tools:

- Step 1: Assess the maturity of your current BA practice standards.

- Step 2: Develop a two-year roadmap and 12-month plan to close gaps and build effective, lean BA practices.

- Step 3: Conduct periodic BA practice maturity assessments and BA workforce capability assessments.

In days gone by, we always followed the maxim, *process first, then tools.* The good news is that BA tools have grown up. Good BA standards are now embedded in integrated requirements management tools. The tools help educate BAs on best practices, integrate and manage requirements knowledge and artifacts, and integrate engineering information into BA artifacts that can be used (and reused) to build solutions. The bad news is that most BAs still use desktop tools that are difficult to maintain and are not integrated. As a result, the BA is burdened with creating, maintaining, integrating, and synchronizing business strategies, goals, models, documents, matrices, use cases, user stories, test cases, etc. Sophisticated tools should be adopted to maintain reusable requirement artifacts, impose standards, and enable education of your BA team.

An organization is only as good as its practices. To be able to make the necessary changes to business analysis in an organization, it is critical to understand the organization's key processes and to adopt a continuous improvement mindset. New/improved BA processes need to "fit" well with existing processes and methods.

STEP 1: ASSESS THE MATURITY OF YOUR CURRENT BA PRACTICE STANDARDS

To determine the current state of your BA practice maturity, conduct an assessment of the BA methods and tools your organization uses; you can then begin to build from the current foundation. At this point you should have a number of BAs capable of performing projects at all levels of complexity: (1) low complexity, (2) moderately complex, and (3) highly complex projects/programs. Perhaps your organization also needs BAs who can perform at the highest level: (4) highly complex program/megaprojects aimed at bringing about breakthrough innovation.

The next step is to determine which practices, both formal and informal, your BA team currently uses. If your BA practices are not documented, ask your team of BAs to work together to document the practices they are using or have used to perform their work for each of the four project levels of complexity, including:

- BA policies, methods, processes, and procedures

- BA requirements management tools, templates, and job aids

- BA manager tools, templates, and the oversight process.

A View from on the Ground

REQUIREMENTS STANDARDS

Kate Gwynne
Associate Director, Business Analysis
Advertising Industry

Capture the current BA methods used in a simple table so that your team can easily and consistently communicate your BA standards to all stakeholders. Use simple communication tools to spread the word about your BA standards. Here's an example:

Type of Requirements Currently Used for Our Projects				
Requirement	What is it?	For example . . .	How is it documented?	Who needs it?
Business requirement	A business requirement is a high level business rationale that addresses our client's need to increase revenue, decrease expenses, drive more people to a site, promote a product, improve customer service, etc.	Client X needs to be informed of inappropriate content in areas where end-users have the ability to provide on-screen images, messages, feedback, and comments.	A business requirements document (BRD) is used to document high level business objectives and requirements.	Entire project team
User Story	A user story is a one-sentence value statement from the user's perspective. "As a _____, I want _____ in order to_____." User stories focus on the people side of a system, but they can be broken down into: User Action > System Response	"As a site visitor, I want the ability to flag inappropriate content." "As a content manager, I want all flagged comments to be forwarded to my Outlook Inbox."	User stories can be documented together or separately, depending on whether the team is working in an agile or waterfall mode.	Entire project team

Functional requirement	Functional requirements are the features of a system. It's how a system functions: the actions, tasks, and behaviors that users interact with. Functional requirements are specific, measurable statements that are traceable back to the user stories or business requirements. Functional requirements should be SMART (specific, measureable, accurate, relevant, and traceable).	You don't need user stories to elicit functional requirements, but it helps if you know how the users want to interact with the system. For example, based on the business requirement and user stories above: | User Action	System Response
The user clicks on Submit Comment.	A red flag icon appears to the right of the text.
The user clicks the red flag icon.	The associated comment disappears from the screen.
The user clicks the red flag icon.	The system sends a notification e-mail to: abc@123.com | Functional requirements identify how the system is going to satisfy the user stories or business requirements.	Sometimes functional requirements are documented in a software requirements specification (SRS). Other times, when images are available, an "annotated creative" is used to reflect functionality.	Technology

Non-functional requirement	Non-functional requirements are performance and maintenance type requirements—things you can't see but know have to be there for the system to run effectively. They include design constraints, external interfaces, metrics, and hosting constraints.	Technology-supported includes: IE 8, 9 iPhone with iOS 5 Android 2.3, 4.0, 4.1 The API will update every 15 minutes to load session detail information.	Non-functional requirements are documented in an SRS or listed in the technology section of an annotated creative.	Technology

It is helpful to use a BA maturity model to perform the current-state maturity assessment. The model is structured into four levels (see Figure 5-1).

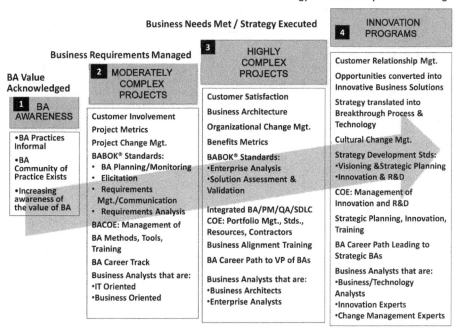

FIGURE 5-1. BA Practice Maturity Model

© 2012 Kathleen Hass and Associates, Inc.

The BA practices required for each level are presented in Table 5-1. Use this matrix as a checklist to help your BA team conduct an assessment and identify gaps that need to be closed.

	Level 1 BA Awareness	Level 2 BA Framework	Level 3 Business Alignment	Level 4 Business/Technology Optimization
Business Outcomes Practices	BA Value Acknowledged	Business Requirements Managed	Business Needs Met Strategy Executed	Technology Used as a Competitive Advantage New Strategy Forged
Customer Relationship Management		Customers and stakeholders are involved throughout the project.	Customer satisfaction is measured for both the process used to involve customers and the new business solution delivered by the project.	External customer relationships and partnerships are measured and managed to continually increase customer satisfaction.

	Level 1 BA Awareness	Level 2 BA Framework	Level 3 Business Alignment	Level 4 Business/Technology Optimization
Standards, Methodology, Tools, Knowledge Management, Change Management	Process and tool standards are undefined.	• BA standards for practices and tools are defined and integrated. • Project knowledge is accessible to all project stakeholders. • Project scope changes are managed.	• BA standards, tools, and knowledge management are integrated with PM, QA, SDLC standards • Organizational readiness assessments are conducted and transition requirements are developed prior to deployment of new solutions.	• Business opportunities are converted into innovative business solutions. • Strategies are translated into breakthrough process and technology change. • Benchmarking, competitive analysis, and feasibility analysis are conducted as part of the strategic planning process. • Cultural readiness assessments are conducted prior to deployment of new transformative solutions.
Body of Knowledge Areas		Standards for the following knowledge areas are defined, institutionalized, and measured: • BA planning and monitoring • Elicitation • Requirements management and communication • Requirements analysis.	Standards for the following knowledge areas are defined, institutionalized, and measured: • Enterprise analysis • Solution assessment and validation.	Standards for the following knowledge areas are defined, institutionalized, and measured: • Strategy formation • R&D • Creativity and innovation • Competitive analysis • Breakthrough process and product design.
Project Selection and Prioritization			• The business and technology architectures are defined and in sync • The portfolio management process ensures business alignment of projects.	• New strategy is formed • Current projects are realigned to new strategy • New initiatives are examined • Business cases are developed to propose new initiatives.

	Level 1 BA Awareness	Level 2 BA Framework	Level 3 Business Alignment	Level 4 Business/Technology Optimization

Metrics		• Project metrics for cost, time, and scope are collected, analyzed, and reported.
		• Requirements defects are tracked, measured, and steps are taken for prevention in the future.
			• Quantitative BA process management program exists and is integrated with PM, QA, SDLC.
			• Business benefits management program is defined and in place.
			• Business value of new solutions is measured and reported.
				• Business benefits management program is tied to the portfolio management program
				• Critical measures include:
				  - Value to customer
				  - Wealth to the bottom line.

Practice Support and Governance	BA forum or community of practice exists.	BACOE: Centralized management of BA standards framework.	BACOE: Centralized management of: • Business case development, portfolio management, BPM, BDM • Resources, contractors, vendors • Governance committee.	BACOE: • Integrated with PM, QA, SDLC COEs • Centralized management of innovation and R&D.
Training and Support		BA standards framework training program exists and all BAs attend.	• All BAs attend business alignment training program.	• All BAs attend business/technology optimization training program. • BA training ROI is measured.
Competency and Career Development		BA career track exists for: • IT oriented analysts • Business-oriented analysts.	BA career path leading to VP of business analysis exists for: • Business architecture analysts • Enterprise business analysts.	BA career path leading to strategic and domain expert BAs exists for: • Business/technology analysts • Cross-functional analysts • Cross-domain analysts • Organizational change analysts • Innovation analysts.

TABLE 5-1. BA Practice Maturity Model Competencies by Level

© 2012 Kathleen Hass and Associates, Inc.

STEP 2: DEVELOP A TWO-YEAR ROADMAP AND 12-MONTH PLAN TO CLOSE GAPS AND BUILD EFFECTIVE, LEAN BA PRACTICES

Working with your BA team, develop a roadmap to refine/adopt/develop practices that are missing from your practice, moving from left to right on the BA practice maturity model. Once your plan has been created (remember, lean, *just enough* investment in BA process and deliverables):

- Update the BA practice business case with new information learned from the assessment

- Include the business benefits of all major milestones

- Gain consensus and approval from your steering committee and executive sponsor for the budget and resources to implement the two-year roadmap and 12-month plan to close gaps in BA practices.

A View from on the Ground

VALUE-BASED BA PRACTICE IMPLEMENTATION ROADMAP

Kate Gwynne

Associate Director, Business Analysis
Advertising Industry

Develop simple and straightforward communication tools to foster consistency of messages about your current practices. Include all implementation plans for establishing the BACOE, building your capable BA team, and closing the gaps on your BA standards.

BA Practice Implementation 12-Month Roadmap
Initiatives for Defining, Guiding, and Building the Business Analysis Practice Standards

DEFINE	**Planning and Communication** ✓ Determine current and future state of BA practice within organization (people, processes, and tools) ✓ Develop business case for future state (people, processes, and tools) ✓ Develop BA practice roadmap (activities and timeline) ✓ Establish analyst advisory group (change leaders) ✓ Develop and implement communication plan for every step in roadmap (include RACI matrix) **Skills and Competency Assessment** ✓ Utilize BA competency profile (IIBA) to determine role level skills and competencies ✓ Determine if roles and skills support project objectives across departments and project types ✓ Establish or update BA role descriptions for each skill level ✓ Administer skills and competency assessment for BA employees ✓ Update interview questions to match skills and competencies for new employees and contractors

GUIDE	**Goals and Career Path Development**
	✓ Review individual assessment results and meet with BAs to establish quarterly and annual goals
	✓ Determine individual training and development plans based on skill needs and career path goals
	Training and Development
	✓ Develop courses and curriculum (or establish vendor relationship for external training)
	✓ Determine informal training opportunities (staff meetings, webinars, books)
	✓ Determine formal training opportunities (IIBA meetings, seminars, conferences)
	✓ Develop new-hire orientation materials for on-boarding BAs
	Knowledge Sharing
	✓ Schedule lunch-n-learn sessions for various audiences to help educate on project best practices and role of BA
	✓ Identify coaching / mentoring opportunities between Junior and Senior analysts
	✓ Develop intranet site for hosting
	   ✓ Webinars, white papers, and links to resources
	   ✓ Templates and process documentation
	   ✓ Calendar of events
	   ✓ Newsletters or blogging

BUILD	**Requirements Management** ✓ Identify metrics to determine key performance indicators and critical success factors for reducing rework ✓ Work with QA to establish ways to track requirements management effectiveness across various project types and departments ✓ Establish key reports to help monitor progress and identify emerging trends **Tools and Technology** ✓ Conduct audit for tools and activities used to manage requirements ✓ Create or modify templates and processes to build efficiencies ✓ Automate manual activities for improved consistency and traceability
MEASURE SUCCESS	**Value to Customers** ✓ % increase in customer satisfaction ✓ % increase in customer retention **Wealth to the Bottom Line** ✓ % reduction in rework costs ✓ % increase in employee satisfaction ✓ % increase in employee retention **Improvement to Project Performance** ✓ Deliver value 100% earlier ✓ 80% on time, budget, scope

STEP 3: CONDUCT PERIODIC BA PRACTICE MATURITY ASSESSMENTS AND BA WORKFORCE CAPABILITY ASSESSMENTS

In your two-year plan, be sure to include periodic assessments of both BA workforce capabilities and the maturity of BA practices. Identify gaps in capabilities and standards and update your two-year roadmap and 12-month plans at least annually to put your organization on the path to continuous improvement. The assessments can be conducted by the BACOE staff.

A View from on the Ground

EXECUTIVE COMMUNICATION TOOL: CURRENT AND FUTURE STATE

Kate Gwynne
Associate Director, Business Analysis
Advertising Industry

Before you begin implementing new BA practices, it is important to understand what the landscape looks like today. We took a look at the people, processes, and tools/technology that will be impacted by these initiatives and identified what's working and what isn't. This varied from department to department, but gave us a good idea of how to move forward in manageable steps.

Here's an example of a useful tool for showing sponsors and executives your journey: "Here's where we are today. Here's where we want to be tomorrow. And here's how we'll get there."

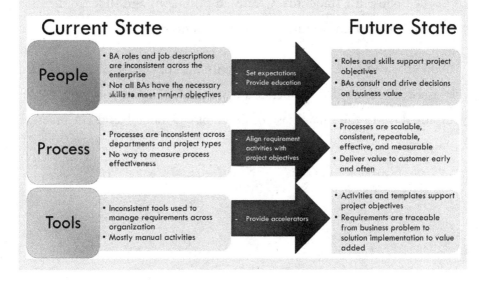

PUTTING IT ALL TOGETHER

WHAT DOES THIS MEAN FOR THE BUSINESS ANALYST?

As a capable BA, you need to have some standard tools in your arsenal. It is important to modify your methods, style, and facilitation techniques as you grow along the maturity spectrum. Always use business language rather than technical IT jargon. Use simple models, drawings, charts, and graphs whenever possible to bring the requirements into view as a way to get your stakeholders to think visually.

WHAT DOES THIS MEAN FOR THE BA MANAGER/PRACTICE LEAD?

Use the experience and talent of your BA team to assess, develop, and improve BA practices. Focus on all aspects of the practice, including people, process, and tools. Resist the temptation to assign one staff person to develop all the BA standards. You want your BA team to take ownership and consequently use the standards. Create simple graphs and slides to describe your path from current to future-state BA practices.

Now that you have put your BA practice into operation and established the infrastructure needed to operate a mature BA practice, it is time to turn your attention to the final phase of developing a value-based BA practice: sustainability.

PART III
Sustainability: It's All About the Value

N ow that you are beginning to put your BA practice into operation, what's next? Step back and review your progress to date. Be sure you have demonstrated that you and your organization are prepared by completing the steps in the readiness phase:

1. Developing the business case for a BA practice

2. Securing a BA practice sponsor who has taken on accountability for the budget and business benefits of a mature BA practice as forecast in the business case

3. Establishing a BA practice steering committee or guidance team composed of influential individuals within your organization who can add clout and political cover

4. Firmly establishing the role of BA practice lead.

Also be sure you have begun to establish the infrastructure needed to operate a mature BA practice by completing the elements of the implementation phase, thereby setting the initial iteration of your practice infrastructure in motion:

- The BA Center of Excellence or similar community of practice

- A capable BA team

- Effective BA standards.

As challenging as these activities have been, the real work lies ahead. To build a lasting BA practice, significant attention needs to be paid to sustainability. The ongoing sustainability phase answers the question, "How do we institutionalize and continue to improve BA practices?"

All too often, new practices remain in place as long as those who developed and implemented them are involved, but then gradually erode over time. Some commonly accepted methods can help you ensure that processes implemented for the value-based BA practice remain strong and effective. For example, ongoing process improvement and management principles can be introduced and sustained by:

- Monitoring BA practice performance against customer-driven process measures

- Certifying the BA practice (ensuring that it meets a set of effectiveness criteria)

- Appointing a process owner who is responsible on an ongoing basis for process performance (in this case, the BA manager/practice lead)

- Ensuring a plan and budget for ongoing improvement of the BA practice

- Creating a reward system that encourages BA practice effectiveness

- Managing between interdependent functions (e.g., project management, business architecture, business process) to build and sustain an aligned organization.

In this part, we discuss important strategies to sustain and continually improve your BA practices. We offer suggestions on the following critical success factors:

- Running Your BA Practice like a Business (Chapter 6)

- Measuring the Effectiveness of Your BA Practice (Chapter 7)

- Focusing on Innovation (Chapter 8)

- Changing the Way We Do Projects (Chapter 9)

- Executing Well-Planned Strategic Communications (Chapter 10)

- Taking your BA Team from Good to Great (Chapter 11).

CHAPTER 6
Running Your BA Practice Like a Business

As organizations navigate the 21st century challenges of constant change, hyperconnectedness, and the critical need for innovation, your BA practice group will need to establish itself as a vital organizational force. Your BA practice is essentially a small business that needs to create value for the organization and its customers.

The good news is that you have made a great start; the bad news is that the real work—the work to ensure sustainability, continuous improvement, and delivery of real business benefits—lies ahead. How do you build a BA practice to last? Your focus at this point is on running the business for the long haul through:

- *Visioning.* Review and update your vision, mission, core values, goals, and objectives for the BA practice as your organization changes and as your practice evolves.

- *Planning.* Develop strategies, plans, and budgets tied to your company's plans and budgets.

- *Business modeling*. Discover and align your plans to the optimal business model for your practice.

- *Growing*. Continually increase the capabilities of your BA team and the maturity of your BA practices.

- *Valuing*. Measure the business benefits of your BA practice and of projects supported by the BA team in terms of value to your customers and wealth to the bottom line.

VISIONING: THE INSPIRATION FOR YOUR BA PRACTICE

Annually revisit and validate the vision, mission, core values, goals, and objectives for the BA practice laid out in your business case. These must be in direct alignment with your organization. Update as needs change. Communicate these every chance you get. Use the vision, mission, core values, goals, and objectives you developed to guide your decisions.

PLANNING: THE BEACON FOR YOUR JOURNEY

Strategic thinking and planning are an art and a science. Your BA practice will thrive if you engage your key supporters and your BAs in strategy discussions often. Develop a lean, fluid, flexible strategic plan and change course as events occur. It is likely that your company has a strategic plan. Whether it is a vibrant strategy or one that is simply written and in resting mode, strive for alignment.

Traditional strategic planning is a comprehensive process for determining what your BA practice should become and how it can best achieve that vision. It appraises the full potential of your practice and links the practice objectives to the organizational strategy—and to the actions your team must take to achieve them. It is a systematic process that helps you ask and answer the most critical questions confronting your practice team.

A traditional strategic planning process involves numerous steps—many of which will have already been completed and captured in your BA practice business case and your BACOE charter and plans. These steps include the following:

- Reviewing your BA practice mission, vision, and core values

- Identifying customer groups (business units, programs, strategic projects) for your BA practice services; understanding the current and future priorities of targeted customer segments

- Defining stakeholder expectations and establishing clear and compelling objectives for each targeted segment

- Analyzing the strengths and weaknesses of the BA practice and determining how you will close the capability gaps

- Identifying and evaluating alternative strategies and approaches

- Developing a value-based business model that will differentiate your BA practice

- Preparing programs, policies, and plans to implement the strategy

- Establishing supportive (but lean) organizational structures, decision processes, information and control systems, and hiring and training systems

- Allocating resources to develop critical capabilities

- Planning for and responding to contingencies or environmental changes

- Monitoring performance.

Flowing from your strategic plans is a one-year business plan and budget, which should be renewed annually. Conduct business planning sessions with your most passionate BAs. Then add key members of your steering committee to perform another review and refinement. The plans don't need to be very detailed (in fact, a higher level provides more flexibility), but they do need to contain "SMART" objectives and clearly state how you will achieve the objectives. SMART objectives are:

- Specific

- Measurable

- Attainable/achievable

- Relevant

- Time-bound.

Resist the temptation to just update your budget from the prior year without first putting together your business plan. Going through the planning steps will enable you to deliberate and explore innovative approaches for the year ahead. Your budget should include salaries plus benefits and bonuses, tools, devices, subscriptions, memberships, seminars and conferences, training, consulting services, website development/upkeep, and other communications media.

A business plan for a BA practice might look something like this:

- Executive Summary
    - o An overview of the BA practice
    - o Who we are:
        - BA consultants

- Management and administration
- Steering committee
- Sponsor
  - o Core values, vision, mission
  - o What products and services we provide
  - o The customers of our products and services
  - o Brief history

- Target Market
  - o Highly complex initiatives, programs, and projects designed to bring about innovation
  - o Areas/business units/functions of the company that are undergoing significant change

- Strategy
  - o Strategic plan summary
  - o Business model
  - o Value proposition

- Implementation Plan
  - o Marketing plan
  - o Communication plan
  - o Change management plan
  - o Partnerships

- Financial Plan
  - o HR/staffing plan
  - o Scope of work forecast
  - o Budget.

MODELING: THE BLUEPRINT OF YOUR PRACTICE

You will probably want to perform business modeling first or midstream in your planning cycle so that you can leverage what you learn. The only way you will be able to determine the optimal business model for your BA practice is to examine your practice elements and map them together. Consider using a tool like the Business Model Canvas *(www.businessmodelgeneration.com/canvas)*, ideally in a group brainstorming session where the key elements of the BA practice are examined and mapped together.

The Business Model Canvas is a visual chart—a blueprint of your BA practice—with elements describing your value proposition, infrastructure, customers, and finances. It will assist you in aligning your activities and conducting trade-off analysis.

GROWING: CONTINUALLY INCREASE THE MATURITY OF YOUR BA PRACTICE

Converting the BA practice maturity model described in detail in Chapter 5 into a roadmap (see Figure 6-1) provides a solid footing as you build on your BA practices. Undoubtedly, you will discover practices in place at all four levels. It is important to realize that practices at higher levels are at risk if lower level practices are not in place and functioning well.

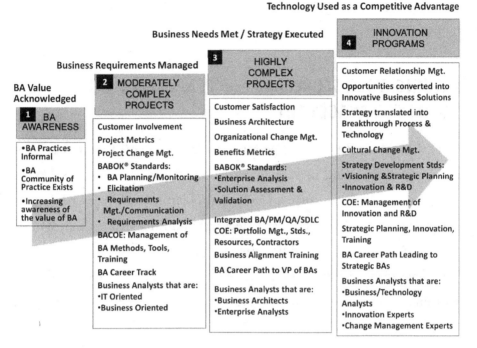

FIGURE 6-1.   BA Practice Maturity Roadmap

©2012 Kathleen Hass and Associates, Inc.

In the absence of a formal maturity assessment, it is difficult to know the current state of the maturity of your BA practices. Fortunately, research provides an industry benchmark that you can use as a starting baseline. The study, *The Bottom Line on Project Complexity,*[1] discovered that current practices are almost mature enough to be consistently successful on moderately complex projects—level 2 in the maturity roadmap. If you assume that your maturity level falls close to the industry benchmark identified in the research, it is likely that your organization has significant gaps for highly complex projects at level 3. The study indicates that these projects are likely to be at least 10 percent and sometimes more than 30 percent over schedule and budget and have a significant reduction in scope. Begin to work to close the gaps, first at level 2 and then at level 3 in the BA practice maturity model.

VALUING: YOUR SCORECARD FOR PERFORMANCE AND STRATEGY MANAGEMENT

Develop your BA practice performance report aligned to your strategy and business plan and to your organization's corporate scorecard. Update and publish it monthly to all critical stakeholders, especially your BA team, BA practice executive sponsor, and steering committee. It should contain all your SMART objectives and performance measures so you will know when your objectives have been met. The BA practice scorecard will help you measure, monitor, and communicate your progress toward strategic goals and performance milestones.

The traditional measures of project success have been performance to schedule, budget, and scope. However, the most important measure of project success is the business benefits realized after the new business solution is deployed.

Ideally, your BAs have been continually updating and validating the assumptions and predictions contained in the business case for their projects, and you have been doing the same with your BA practice business case. Ultimately, business benefits are measured in terms of value to the customer and wealth to the bottom line.

For your most important projects, you can take several steps to ensure that you are able to measure the ultimate value of the business benefits of projects, which is the key responsibility of business analysts:

- If you don't have a business case for your critical projects, call together a small expert team to build the business case. Identify all costs, including the cost to operate the new/changed business solution. Then, predict business benefits in terms of customer value and bottom-line results.

- Present the business benefits predicted in the business case to the executive sponsor of the project and ask, "Does this accurately describe the benefits you are expecting from this project?"

- Determine how to measure value to the customer and wealth (revenue vs. cost) from the deployed solution.

- Continue to validate and update the business case throughout the project. If the case begins to erode, reconvene the expert team to review options, restate the business case, and recommend the most feasible change in course to the executive sponsor.

- After the new solution is deployed, the BA serves as a business realization manager. Measure the value of the new solution, making improvements and adjustments to how it is used to optimize business benefits.

We close this chapter with a view from an experienced and highly successful executive who has a keen awareness of how to be successful when delivering business analysis services in various settings. As a consultant, Michael Augello has seen it from both sides: running a BA consultancy business and running a BA practice within a company. Consider his insightful advice as you build your sustainability plans and approach.

A View from on the Ground

THE BUSINESS OF BUSINESS ANALYSIS

Michael Augello

BA Practice Consultant and Entrepreneur

Taking the personal risk of creating one's own company requires courage, passion, belief in a vision, and an understanding of what success looks like. Running an internal BA practice is no different. A strong focus on several elements is critical for success:

- Vision
- Business plan
- Services
- People, process, and tools
- Business practices.

Vision

Vision is a critical element of success.

1. *It's about value*—utter belief in the end game value and the positive outcomes the BA practice will deliver.

2. *Team vision alignment*—ability to articulate that value in simple, concise language that everyone in your team understands, believes, and sees. Your BA team must understand and share your belief. Team belief builds resilience in the face of adversity.

3. *Stakeholder/client alignment*—ability to articulate that value in simple, concise language that all external stakeholders/potential clients understand, believe in, and want for their own organization. They must understand and share the belief.

BA practices fail (or are at considerable risk) if the BA practice lead does not have vision alignment or is unable to "brand" it far and wide. The challenge is to continually communicate your vision and bring only people who share the vision into your team. In successful businesses this seems to be easy, since the founders typically are driven in their pursuit of the vision and it often becomes part of their DNA. In the business of running an internal BA practice, the communication of the vision—the brand—is equally important.

Business Plan

Some entrepreneurs develop their business plan and business model in their heads; others write it down in various degrees of detail. If external financing is involved, the entrepreneur is forced to record business plans and business models to satisfy investors and bankers.

In the domain of the BA practice manager/leader, developing plans and demonstrating value are essential to earn organizational support. Most organizations require a feasibility document or a business case supported by an executive presentation. The business plan needs to be revisited each year for the practice to continually demonstrate value. Perhaps more important is the ability to present your case with passion and conviction in language that all stakeholders understand.

Services

In a consulting business, as well as in an internal BA practice, answers to the following questions must be crystal clear:

- What is the client buying? What are the services? What will they be receiving?
- What value will they derive? What is the cost versus benefit for the client?
- Can I deliver? Do I have the quality? Can I exceed client expectations?

- Do I have the right people? What support do my people need?

- Can I cover my costs? Can I make a profit/demonstrate value? What is the cost versus benefit for my business/practice?

- Does my team believe in the client? Does my team believe in the project? Do they understand their role? Do they feel empowered? Do they have the ability to exceed expectations?

People, Process, and Tools

The people on your team are your most important asset, and your customers are your most important stakeholders. Take exceptional care of your people, demonstrate real value to your customers, and referrals and repeat business will flow your way.

- *People.* Hire only empowered, passionate, disciplined people. Stay very close to your team. They represent your company, your brand, and your practice.

- *Customer service.* Being generous with your time is an attitude; being a genuine person is an attitude. Providing customer service when running your own business requires an indisputably positive attitude. A BA practice must excel at customer service.

- *Process.* Focus on quality, people support, technical and emotional support, and unwavering attention to detail in terms of quality in every aspect of the practice to exceed customers' expectations.

- *Tools.* Tools will free your BAs from documentation maintenance and enable them to operate as real consultants.

Business Practices

Running your BA practice like a business requires attention to the "business" of the business analysis practice. Focus on your strengths and engage specialists to free you to focus on your people, the deliverables, and your customers.

Financial management of a private business is quite similar to balancing the BA practice group's budget. Always demonstrate the value your BA practice is contributing to your business unit and to the organization as a whole. The budget format for the BA practice should mirror that of the unit or company. Proactively engage the accounting specialists in your organization to help implement the financial systems to run the practice.

Compliance with HR, legal, accounting, and government regulations is critical for businesses; similarly, the BA practice's adherence to organizational compliance rules is critical to survival. Proactively engage specialists in your organization to keep you one step ahead of tomorrow's problem.

Set the BA practice up, run it like a business, and it will perform!

PUTTING IT ALL TOGETHER

WHAT DOES THIS MEAN FOR THE BUSINESS ANALYST?

For the individual BA, consider these strategies:

- Make sure you have a valid business case for your project.

- Ensure that you can measure business benefits after the solution is delivered.

- Work with your BA practice lead and BA team to improve BA practice maturity.

- Make sure you have the right people on your project.

WHAT DOES THIS MEAN FOR THE BA MANAGER/PRACTICE LEAD?

It is imperative for your BA practice sustainability that you run your practice like a business. Examine your organization's strategy and determine how your BA practice contributes toward advancing that strategy. Focus on real financial measurements—those of concern to your executive management team. If your organization has a corporate scorecard, provide your measurements in the same or a similar format. Work with the BAs on critical projects to ensure that they are focusing on value to the customer and wealth to the bottom line.

The best way to visualize what it would be like to run your BA practice like a business is to examine an award-winning, world class business specializing in business analysis. Redvespa (*http://redvespa.com*) is just such a business— and an exceptional example. See the case study following the Epilogue for a description of Redvespa's best practices, which apply to any BA practice.

Chapter 7 discusses additional strategies for measuring the value and quality of your BA practice.

NOTES

1   *The Bottom Line on Project Complexity*, conducted by Kathleen B. Hass and Lori Lindbergh, PhD, presented at the PMI Global Congress 2010 North America. The study correlated the current state of BA practice maturity with project complexity and project outcomes.

CHAPTER 7
Measuring the Effectiveness of Your BA Practice

To establish a BA practice that lasts, you must demonstrate value. Developing measures of success and reporting progress to executives will demonstrate the value that business analysis adds to the organization. As we have discussed, the ultimate measures of business analysis success are value to the customer and wealth to the bottom line of your organization. On the path to achieving these benefits, your stakeholders will be looking for other measures of the BA practice's success, including the following:

- Project performance measures

- Quality performance measures

- BA process performance measures.

PROJECT PERFORMANCE MEASURES

Project performance is typically measured in terms of adherence to cost, time, and scope estimates. One test of the success of the BA practice is improvements in these measures. Compare the forecasts with actual results for projects that are working with a business analyst and quantify the improvements to demonstrate the value your BAs have contributed.

PROJECT TIME AND COST OVERRUN IMPROVEMENTS

Quantify project time and cost overruns prior to implementation of BA practices, and compare with those projects that are supported by the BA practice. If a baseline measurement is not available in your organization, use industry standard benchmarks. Other measures might be improvements to team member morale and reduction in project staff turnover.

PROJECT PORTFOLIO VALUE

Prepare reports for the executive team that provide the investment costs and expected value of the portfolio of projects as forecast in the business case; report the actual value that new solutions add to the organization compared to the expected value predicted in the business case.

QUALITY PERFORMANCE MEASURES

Requirements quality validation is the process of evaluating requirements documents and models to determine whether they meet business needs and are complete enough that the technical team can finalize solution design and begin development. Quality validation activities should be part of your standard BA processes. Justify the efforts by demonstrating that defects found and fixed early will be vastly less expensive to fix than those found during testing or in production. Quality defect information provides data to support defect detection and prevention.

DEFECT DETECTION

Validation activities are essential to detect and fix any omissions, errors, or other defects before further investment is made to convert the requirements into working processes and systems. Defects are typically logged into a defect tracking tool and prioritized by severity.

DEFECT PREVENTION

Defect prevention involves a further process to analyze and prevent the occurrence of similar defects in the future. Defect prevention involves a continuous process of collecting defect data, conducting root cause analysis to determine the origin/source of the defects, and implementing corrective actions.

REWORK TIME/COST IMPROVEMENTS

Track the number of requirements defects discovered during testing and after the solution is in production prior to implementation of the BA practice, compared with those projects supported by the BA practice. Quantify the value in terms of reduced rework time and costs and improved customer satisfaction.

QUALITY REVIEWS

Requirements validation activities are usually conducted through quality reviews. Quality review sessions should be conducted in a safe environment; avoid placing blame on the author(s) of the requirements artifacts under review. The validation team compares the set of requirements with the original initiating documents (business case, project charter, or statement of work) to ensure completeness. Include both business and technical representatives in the review process:

- Business representatives focus on the clarity and accuracy of the requirements.

- Technical representatives focus on whether the requirements are sufficient to finalize design and begin development of the business solution.

Beyond establishing completeness, validation activities include evaluating requirements to ensure that design risks associated with the requirements are minimized before further investment is made in developing the solution. An often-used analysis technique to help validate and understand requirements is prototyping, which involves developing a sample or model of the solution to the requirement. Bring developers into the requirements process; use them to build validation prototypes during the requirements elicitation and validation activities.

CHARACTERISTICS OF QUALITY REQUIREMENTS

It may be helpful to use a requirements validation checklist (see Figure 7-1) to review the quality of a set of requirements. The checklist should be tailored for projects of low, moderate, and high complexity and customized based on the specific business and technology domain being addressed.

Quality Review Cover Page:	Requirements Validation Checklist

	Date:
	Attendees:
	• Technical team members:
	• Business team members:
	• Author/BA:
	• Others:
	• Original initiating documents to be used to ensure completeness of requirements:
	  o Business case
	  o Project charter
	  o Statement of work.

ID Number	Quality Characteristic	Explanation	Criteria Met (Y/N)	If No, Defect and Rework Required	Another Review Needed? (Y/N)
	Clear	Requirement is clear and concise so it can be used by virtually everyone on the project. Selected types of requirements are expressed formally using technical language (e.g., legal, safety, security) and they are mapped back to the requirements that are more easily understood. However, in most cases the language used to document requirements is as nontechnical as possible.			
	Unambiguous	The requirement is concisely stated without technical jargon or acronyms (unless defined elsewhere in the requirements document). It expresses objective facts, not subjective opinions, and is subject to only one interpretation. Vague subjects, adjectives, prepositions, verbs, and phrases are avoided, as are negative statements and compound statements.			

ID Number	Quality Characteristic	Explanation	Criteria Met (Y/N)	If No, Defect and Rework Required	Another Review Needed? (Y/N)
	Visible	A diagram can express structure and relationships more clearly than text; for precise definition of concepts, clearly articulated language is superior to diagrams. Therefore, both textual and graphical representations are essential for a complete set of requirements. Transforming graphical requirements into textual form can make them more understandable to nontechnical team members.			
	Unique	The requirement addresses only one thing. Each requirement is unique, describing an exclusive need to be met by the solution. Each requirement has an identifier that does not change. The reference is not reused if the requirement is moved, changed, or deleted.			
	Complete	The requirement is fully stated in one place with no missing information.			
	Consistent	The requirement does not contradict any other requirement and is fully consistent with all authoritative external documentation.			
	Traceable	The requirement meets all or part of a business need as stated by stakeholders and is authoritatively documented.			
	Current	The requirement has not become obsolete.			

ID Number	Quality Characteristic	Explanation	Criteria Met (Y/N)	If No, Defect and Rework Required	Another Review Needed? (Y/N)
	Verifiable	The implementation of the requirement can be determined through inspection, demonstration, test (instrumented), or analysis (including validated modeling and simulation). Acceptance criteria describe the nature of the test that will demonstrate to customers, end users, and stakeholders that the requirement has been met. These criteria are usually captured from the end users by asking the question, "What kind of assessment would satisfy you that this requirement has been met?"			

FIGURE 7-1. Sample BA Quality Assurance Checklist

ATTRIBUTES OF QUALITY REQUIREMENTS

Attributes are used for a variety of purposes, including explaining, selecting, filtering, validating, and assuring quality. Attributes allow the BA team to associate information with individual or related groups of requirements; they often facilitate the requirements analysis process by filtering and sorting. Assessing these attributes during quality reviews is one way to focus on the quality of BA requirements artifacts.

As BA practice lead, build a checklist of the attributes that are most important to your organization. Figure 7-2 is a sample checklist of the attributes that are generally relied on in the BA industry.

ID Number	Quality Attributes	Explanation	Criteria Met (Y/N)	If No, Correction / Refinement Needed	Another Review Needed? (Y/N)
	Complexity Indicator	Indicates how difficult the requirement will be to implement. Highly complex requirements have numerous interdependencies and interrelationships with other requirements. Complex requirements demand more rigor to define and model and more verification to demonstrate their validity.			
	Owner	Specifies the individual or group that needs the requirement. The absence of ownership indicates that the requirement may not be valid.			
	Performance	Addresses how the requirement must be met and how fast the process must be executed.			
	Priority	Rates the relative importance of the requirement based on business value. Low-priority requirements typically have a low return on investment and are likely not produced.			
	Source	Identifies who requested the requirement. Every requirement should originate from a source that has authority to specify requirements.			
	Stability	Indicates how mature the requirement is, in particular, whether the requirement is firm enough to prioritize it and to begin work on it.			
	Status	Denotes whether the requirement is proposed, accepted, verified with the users, or implemented.			

ID Number	Quality Attributes	Explanation	Criteria Met (Y/N)	If No, Correction / Refinement Needed	Another Review Needed? (Y/N)
	Urgency	Refers to how soon the requirement is needed to meet the business objectives, the market window.			
	Functionality	Indicates the requirement can be implemented so that it performs the functions and features needed, and complies with the relevant standards. Issues related to data security are considered.			
	Usability	Indicates the requirement is intuitive, easy to understand, and easy to use. Customers/ users will be able to perform their tasks in a consistent and efficient manner. The solution appears to be simple, hiding the complex technology from the customers/users.			
	Reliability	Indicates a high probability of failure-free operation of a business process in a specified environment for a specified time.			
	Efficiency and Performance	Demonstrates that the requirement can be implemented efficiently in the target environment, performing the tasks in an appropriate timeframe with a reasonable amount of resources.			
	Maintainability	Indicates the level of difficulty to maintain, enhance, and refine the requirement as business need changes.			

FIGURE 7-2. Sample BA Quality Attributes Checklist

BA PROCESS PERFORMANCE MEASURES

Another measure of quality is the effectiveness of the process used to develop the requirements. Your BA team should have a defined process that includes the minimal types and numbers of requirements artifacts for projects of differing complexity. Remember, use "just enough" process. Again, it may be helpful to use a checklist during validation sessions to ensure that your standard process is being followed. Process steps may include the following:

- *Planning* requirements activities, focusing on the number and type of elicitation sessions to be conducted and the requirements artifacts to be produced. Plans should follow your organization's defined standard process. If you plan well and capture actual data on how long it takes to develop, manage changes, and validate requirements for projects of varying complexity, you will have an idea of the appropriate timeline. Require your BAs to develop plans for their activities, capture actuals, and begin to build historical data and a target timeline for projects of varying complexity.

- *Studying* requirements feasibility to determine if requirements are viable technically, operationally, and economically.

- *Trading off* requirements to determine the most feasible alternatives.

- *Assessing* requirements feasibility by analyzing requirements risks and constraints and modifying requirements to mitigate identified risks. The goal is to reduce requirements risks through early validation prototyping techniques.

- *Modeling* requirements to restate and clarify them. Modeling is accomplished at the appropriate usage, process, or detailed structural level.

- *Deriving* additional requirements as more is learned about the business need.

- *Prioritizing* requirements to reflect that not all requirements are of equal value to the business. Prioritization is essential to determine the level of effort, budget, and time required to provide the highest priority functionality first. Perhaps lower priority needs can be addressed in a later release of the system.

A View from on the Ground

FOCUS ON MOST VALUABLE ACTIVITIES

Barbara A. Carkenord

Author, Educator

Training and Consulting Industry

One of the biggest advantages of business analysis thinking is helping others prioritize. BAs look for business value in every task and in every project. They recognize that some work is more valuable to the organization than other work. BAs can be a great help with time management—for themselves and their coworkers. BAs decide to work on the most important and valuable tasks each day and can help others in the organization make good decisions about where to spend their limited time. Keeping the organization focused on the most important tasks minimizes waste and increases success.

PUTTING IT ALL TOGETHER

WHAT DOES THIS MEAN FOR THE BUSINESS ANALYST?

For the individual BA, consider these strategies:

- In the absence of organizational requirements validation checklists, build and use your own.

- Work with your PM to include time to conduct quality reviews into the project schedule.

- Work with your BA practice lead and BA team to improve the quality of your BA deliverables.

WHAT DOES THIS MEAN FOR THE BA MANAGER/PRACTICE LEAD?

For the BA practice lead, consider these strategies:

- Develop requirements validation checklists for low complexity, moderately complex, and highly complex projects and programs.

- Ensure that all BAs follow the quality assurance processes.

- Begin to collect basic data on the time, resources, and quality of your BA practices using the completed checklists and BA plans so that you can report improvements realized from business analysis.

For BAs to reach their full potential and add significant value to their organizations, they need to become masters at creative leadership of innovative change. In Chapter 8, we focus on how BAs can develop innovative solutions that help their organizations bring value to their customers and wealth to their bottom lines.

CHAPTER 8
Focusing on Innovation

n this complex, highly competitive global economy, your organizational change initiatives need to produce innovative solutions. Incremental changes to "business as usual" are no longer enough for organizations to remain viable. Yet, many CEOs do not believe they have the creative leadership needed to capitalize on complexity and bring about innovation.[1]

The pressure to innovate is not just for high tech companies. All organizations that are trying to do more with less while struggling to stay competitive are under pressure to innovate. Some believe that innovation is simply another business process that will become institutionalized, like financial management and strategic planning. But while organizations of all kinds need to innovate for survival, few are able to make innovation a reality. Those that do innovate are richly rewarded.

So what does innovation have to do with business analysis? For BAs to reach their full potential and add significant value to their organizations, they need to become masters at creative leadership of innovative change. Traditional BA activities are still important, but we must change how we do business analysis. The focus on innovation in the 21st century is a call to action for business analysts.

EMBRACE CREATIVE LEADERSHIP

Serving as a key project leader with a constant focus on adding value to the business, the business analyst is positioned to be a powerful influencer of change. The BA is coming to the forefront of project management to close the gaps in areas that have historically been overlooked in mission-critical business transformation initiatives. Areas in the purview of the business analyst that require focused attention for projects to produce real business value include the following:

- Conducting *enterprise analysis* with an expert team whose members have diverse backgrounds and capturing the details about the most valuable opportunities in a business case by:

  o Defining business problems and identifying new business opportunities for achieving innovation and remaining competitive

  o Understanding the business and the effects of proposed solutions across the enterprise

  o Insisting on innovation, fostering creativity, rejecting business as usual, and welcoming ambiguity and disruptive change

  o Maintaining an intense focus on the business benefits the initiative is expected to bring to the enterprise in terms of value to customers and wealth to the bottom line

  o Validating that the new solution capitalizes on the opportunity and will contribute the expected business benefits

  o Managing the benefits expected from the new solution during and after project completion.

- Translating the business objectives into business requirements using powerful modeling visualization tools.

For BAs to become creative leaders of innovative change, they must operate at the enterprise level and engage in holistic thinking, business outcome thinking, and strategy execution through creative solutions. BAs need to view themselves as creative change agents, visionaries, and credible leaders.

WELCOME CHANGE

The prevalence of large-scale organizational change has grown exponentially in the 21st century. All indications are that change—big change—is here to stay. As the rate of change increases, the willingness and ability of BAs to acquire new expertise and skills are central to their career success and their organization's continued viability. BAs who are able to develop the capacity to navigate a complex, uncertain, and dynamic business environment and truly innovate are vital to their organization's survival. Businesses are counting on BAs to advance innovation through organizational transformation and to become creative leaders of innovative change.

CREATING AND SUSTAINING THE VISION

Successful change is anchored in a compelling vision. A common vision of change objectives and the resulting business benefits is essential for a team to bring about significant and sometimes disruptive innovation. A clear vision helps direct, align, and inspire team members. Without a clear vision, a lofty transformation plan can be reduced to a list of inconsequential projects that sap energy and drain valuable resources. Most important, a clear vision guides decision-making so that people do not arrive at every decision through unnecessary debate and conflict. As a BA leading change, insist on a common vision, revisit it often, and use it to drive decision-making.

BUILDING YOUR CREDIBILITY

When acting as a change agent, the business analyst and BA practice manager/leader need to develop and sustain a high level of credibility, which is built on trustworthiness and expertise. Above all, a business analyst must strive to be a reliable source of information. Professional presence, ethics, and integrity are the cornerstones of credibility.

The business analyst can develop credibility by becoming proficient in these critical skills and competencies, all of which should be part of every BA's professional development plan:

- Practicing business outcome thinking

- Conceptualizing and thinking creatively

- Demonstrating interpersonal skills

- Valuing ethics and integrity

- Using robust communication techniques to keep all stakeholders informed

- Empowering team members and building high-performing teams

- Setting direction and providing vision

- Listening effectively and encouraging new ideas

- Seeking responsibility and accepting accountability

- Focusing and motivating a group to achieve what is important

- Capitalizing on and rewarding the contributions of various team members

- Managing complexity to reduce project risks and to foster creativity

- Welcoming changes that enhance the value of the solution or product.

FOSTER INNOVATION

Business analysts are now being challenged to rethink their approach—to not just record what the business is doing or wants to do, but to operate as a lightning rod to stimulate creativity and innovation. To do so, business analysts are rethinking the role of customers and users, viewing them as creative resources that can contribute imagination and inventiveness as well as operational effectiveness.

Some organizations demand that key employees spend 20 percent of their time investigating new ideas, thinking "out of the box" and "out of the project," even "out of the building." Perhaps 20 percent of a BA's time on a project should be dedicated to innovation—innovation in the way the team works, in the team's interaction with customers and other stakeholders, and of course, in solution design. The business analyst who works across and up and down the organization, getting the right people to the table at the right time and in the right place, can fan the flames of creativity.

There is an emerging trend related to innovation that BAs need to be aware of, and perhaps expert in: *design thinking*. Although it is not novel, design thinking is enjoying a resurgence because of the strong focus on innovation across the competitive landscape. The Institute of Design at Stanford University has become one of the trendy, most talked about purveyors of design thinking. Stanford is spreading the word around the world to improve our lives through collaboration that inspires human-centered innovations.

Design thinking is an approach to combining creative and analytical thinking and applying the results toward solving a specific problem. It is an iterative process that centers on five steps focused on the customer: empathize, define, ideate, prototype, and test. A renewed look at design thinking is catching on quickly. It would serve BAs well to become experts in design thinking

LEVERAGE COMPLEXITY

How does a business analyst bring about innovation in an organizational environment of uncertainty, constant change, and complexity? The beauty of complexity is that it breeds creativity.

Complex systems fluctuate between equilibrium—a state where the system cannot adapt to its surroundings and that leads to paralysis—and chaos, a state where the system is unable to function (see Figure 8-1). The most creative state is on the edge of chaos. Today's BAs are challenged to bring their teams to the edge of chaos, to be "in the zone," where ideas are flowing, people are challenging and building on each other's ideas, and team members are at the white board visualizing what could be. That is when the BA lead sits back and gets out of the way, asking periodically: "Are we truly innovating?" The trick is to get the right people in the room and to establish a safe environment for them to create.

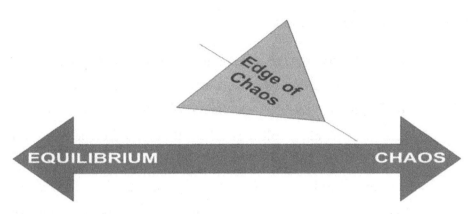

FIGURE 8-1. Edge of Chaos Management

BECOME AN INSPIRING BUSINESS ANALYST

Facilitating groups to solve problems and make decisions in an innovative way is the creative leader's most powerful role, and this is becoming the BA's call to action.

It is a tall order to ask 21st century business analysts and BA practice leads to foster creativity throughout their organizations. Nonetheless, this goal is not as elusive as it seems. Business analysts' expertise in facilitation fosters constructive dialogue, and dialogue cultivates creativity. Creativity-provoking facilitation techniques are designed to discourage teams from jumping immediately to the "right" answer, because there really is no right answer, only the most feasible and most valuable idea we have identified at the moment. The facilitator who fosters creativity strives to be tolerant of, and in fact encourages, unconventional answers, intermittent disruptions, and even diversions, never knowing where they might lead.

CREATIVITY-INDUCING TECHNIQUES

Many of today's great designs have originated from teams using a range of creativity techniques. Be sure you use multiple brainstorming approaches to keep your facilitation fresh. For a simple approach to get you started, consider using the technique called SCAMPER. This technique builds on the premise that most innovations are modifications and combinations of something that already exists. SCAMPER can be used as a checklist of idea-provoking questions. This particular technique is especially effective for product and process design or enhancement. Each letter stands for a different facilitation approach:

- **S**ubstitute
- **C**ombine
- **A**dapt
- **M**ultiply or modify
- **P**ut to other uses
- **E**liminate
- **R**earrange or reverse.[2]

BELIEFS AND BEHAVIORS

Creative leaders have many distinguishing beliefs and observable behavioral characteristics that set them apart from traditional managers and leaders who are focused on efficient operations. See Table 8-1 for just a few.

Leadership Objective	Distinguishing Beliefs and Observable Behaviors
Define what must be done	Establishes breakthrough vision, goals, objectives, strategies: • Envisions the future direction • Focuses on the competition • Aligns with current strategy and forges new directions • Disrupts old markets; creates new ones.
Create networks of collaborators	Aligns teams and stakeholders to the future vision: • Makes customer-focused decisions • Masters positive politics • Gains commitment and secures loyalty • Partners with far-reaching groups; forges public-private partnerships • Collaborates and cooperates outside the business.
Ensure the job gets done	Builds creative teams that are: • Passionate • Highly skilled • Disciplined • High-performing • Trusted • Empowered • Courageous • Innovative • Focused on creating value.
Make decisions that lead to innovation	• Spends time on reflection, thinking, experimenting, brainstorming • Believes that no idea is right or wrong • Resists the temptation to select the final solution too early.
Translate ideas into innovative solutions	• Prototypes in the lab • Experiments in the real world • Seeks feedback constantly • Welcomes changes that add value • Understands that failure is part of the innovation process • Keeps options open until the last responsible moment • Puts the minimal solution into the customer environment to see if it is accepted.
Fearless, audacious	• Is courageous enough to change everything.

TABLE 8-1. Creative Leader Characteristics

KNOWLEDGE, SKILLS, AND METHODS

Innovation, by definition, creates deep, transformative change. Creative BAs develop a unique understanding of innovation and the knowledge, skills and creativity-heightening methods that are needed (see Table 8-2).

Knowledge/Skill/ Method	What It Looks Like
Understand innovation	• Innovation is a team sport that requires collaboration. • Evolutionary innovation improves a product in an existing market. • Disruptive innovation disrupts the existing market.
Understand innovation drivers	These include: • New/changing customer needs and problems • New technologies • New regulations • New competitors.
Understand innovation principles	• Always start with an urgent business need. • Do not think your organization has only one or two innovators. • Get the right people in the room—the best thinkers across your organization. • Explore many ideas. • Get the group to let go of old ideas before you expect them to come up with new ones. • Focus on simple solutions that meet real customer needs. • Create a sense of urgency.
Facilitate constructive dialogue	• Engage in constructive dialogue that leverages creativity in the face of ambiguity, tension, and indecisiveness.
Create an environment of respect	• Ensure that participants are willing to have their ideas and beliefs challenged, examined, and reexamined. • Ensure that participants respect each other and recognize the benefits that come from open, candid, lively discussion.
Think outside the project, outside the organization, outside the industry	• Penetrate the intimidating set of customs that exist in any organization. • Avoid limiting options by focusing on competitors doing comparable things.

Knowledge/Skill/ Method	What It Looks Like
Use creativity-inducing facilitation methods	• Get the right people in the room. • Be open to all ideas. • Timebox sessions. • Get out of the way; let the group do the work. • Control the process, not the people. • Plan and prepare for the session. • Mix up your creativity-inducing techniques. • Have fun.

TABLE 8-2. Creative BA Characteristics

TAP THE WISDOM OF INNOVATION TEAMS

In Chapter 11 we talk about what makes capable teams of all kinds become great teams. When the solution is elusive and innovation is critical, adopt practices learned from organizations that have successfully established special innovation teams—and then get out of the way! Assign a business analyst and project manager who have exceptional technical skills, a highly flexible style, and exceptional relationship-building skills—and are comfortable working with uncertainty. Innovation comes most readily when special teams are established, removed from the day-to-day operations of the business, fully funded, fully supported from the top, and timeboxed. Work with your executive sponsor to foster innovation teams.

Although innovation projects can originate from any business unit, they are often managed through special units that transcend typical organizational/operational boundaries and are focused on breakthrough ideas, emerging markets, and new business ventures. These special teams are flexibly structured and highly connected via the Internet, augmented with periodic face-to-face meetings. To succeed, these groups need executive support from the highest levels of the organization—and full funding. Some organizations establish the innovation teams as a separate division, while others establish one "innovation team" that spans all divisions and works on projects that meet predefined criteria.

NURTURE INNOVATIVE LEADERSHIP

BA managers/leads and on-the-ground BAs can encourage innovation within their organizations and teams in a variety of ways:

- *Promote opportunities for your teams to try new and fun things through idea generation, prototyping, and experimentation.* Involve your developers to help you prototype so they don't get anxious and begin to assume what is needed. Make sure your BAs regularly see innovation displayed in a positive light and are rewarded for their innovative pursuits; they will be much more likely to step out of their comfort zones.

- *Create an environment within your team where problem-solving is encouraged.* While people can and do solve problems innovatively in their personal lives, they don't always feel empowered to make changes when obstacles, difficult personalities, negative reinforcements, or red tape get in the way at work.

- *Encourage diversity and "differentness."* Many of today's famous innovators are people who deviated from the accepted life roadmap. Realize that to innovate, your team may not do things in an expected manner, may deviate from your standards, and may look different than you envision.

IMPLEMENT INNOVATION METRICS

What you measure drives behaviors. However, innovation is one of those things that is difficult to measure. Although there is not a standard measure of innovation, companies are attempting to measure their *innovation quotient*.

Measures of innovation for organizations are often conducted through research, surveys, workshops, consultants, or internal benchmarking. Many businesses have adopted the balanced scorecard approach, which involves business measures related to finances, innovation process efficiency, employees' contributions and motivation, and benefits for customers. Measurements of innovation vary widely, covering revenue from new products, spending in R&D, time to market, customer and employee satisfaction, number of patents, and additional sales resulting from past and new innovations. BA managers/practice leads need to strive to use the measures of innovation that make the most sense in their industry and their environment.

ADOPT NEW TECHNOLOGIES

Perhaps one of the most forward-thinking views on innovation is provided by Ashish Mehta, IIBA Director of Emerging Markets and Regional Director of India. He believes the next-generation business analysts need to familiarize themselves with new technologies and constantly work to incorporate them into their business solution architecture to bring about innovation. Some of these new technologies include the following:

- *Mobility*: providing great flexibility and value in the hands of employees, customers, and partners

- *Social media*: providing instant customer feedback, suggestions, and complaints

- *Big data analytics*: enabling smart decisions based on real-time information

- *Cloud*: making information available anytime, anywhere

- *Gamification*: applying game-design thinking to all critical processes, including employee engagement, new ideas/innovations, training, quality service, and customer feedback.[3]

PUTTING IT ALL TOGETHER

WHAT DOES THIS MEAN FOR THE BUSINESS ANALYST?

Creative leaders produce sustainable change. Strive to become a creative leader—creative leadership is critical to your organization's survival and your career advancement.

Leaders rely on their credibility and ethics to succeed; never sacrifice your integrity. Focus your professional development plan on communications, creativity, innovation, facilitation, team leadership, and influencing skills. Include all types of learning:

- Formal training and certifications

- Informal mentoring

- Experiences that stretch your capabilities

- Self-study

- Reading, reading, reading.

Test the waters. Begin to lead your teams through edge-of- chaos creative sessions at key points in change initiatives:

- Before projects are selected and funded, to propose innovative solutions to complex business problems

- At the beginning of projects, when key experts are in the room, minimally the PM, the BA, the business visionary, and the lead technologist (architect, developer, IT visionary), to validate the business case and make sure you are truly innovating

- At key points throughout the project, perhaps after each major release, to revalidate the business case and make sure you are innovating.

Finally, don't take yourself too seriously. People want to work with leaders who are credible and present themselves well, but they also want to have fun. Learn how to balance seriousness with playful creativity. Spend a lot of time planning your meetings, the techniques you will use, and the outcomes you need. Then take a step back and make sure the experience will be fruitful, rewarding, and fun for all participants.

WHAT DOES THIS MEAN FOR THE BA MANAGER/PRACTICE LEAD?

If you are a BA manager/practice lead, insist that your BAs conduct real enterprise analysis, experimentation, and prototyping to drive innovation before a business case is created and used to propose a new initiative. If your BAs are assigned to a project and these activities have not been adequately performed, help them pull together a small expert team and facilitate them through this important research and analysis. Continually ask: "Are we really innovating?" Study successful innovation teams and strive to establish a truly innovative BA practice. See Appendix B, Innovation Process Checklist, to get you started.

It is not enough to simply talk about innovation. Premier universities around the globe are offering studies on innovation, design, and creativity. Seek out educational opportunities for you and your senior/enterprise BA consultants.

In Chapter 9 we examine the key changes needed in the way we do projects to drive attention toward business benefits, customer value, creativity, and innovation.

NOTES

1   IBM Institute for Business Value, "Capitalizing on Complexity: Insights from the Global Chief Executive Officer Study, 2010. Online at *www.ibm.com/services/us/ceo/ceostudy2010 (accessed February 2014).*

2   Bob Eberle, *Scamper: Creative Games and Activities for Imagination Development* (Waco, TX: Prufrock Press, 2008).

3   Mehta, Ashish, *Next Generation Business Analysis,* Building Business Capability (BBC) Conference, Las Vegas, 2013.

CHAPTER 9
Changing the Way We Do Projects

An organization's culture is durable because it is "the way we do things around here." The BA practice is called upon to shepherd changes to the way organizations select projects, develop and manage requirements, run projects, and determine project success.

The BA practice manager/lead and the team of business analysts are an unstoppable force to change the way we do projects, driving attention toward business benefits, customer value, creativity, and innovation. In this chapter, we examine the key changes needed in the way we do projects to:

- Focus on value-based decision-making

- Relieve the burden of analysis

- Lead projects collaboratively

- Manage complexity

- Maximize business value.

FOCUS ON VALUE-BASED DECISION-MAKING

All project decisions should be based on business value, even for IT projects. This is likely to represent a significant shift in your organization's practices. Many organizational cultures still engage in the practice of piling project requests, accompanied by sparse requirements, onto the IT and new-product development groups and then wondering why they cannot seem to deliver. Moreover, project success is still measured in terms of adherence to cost, time, and scope predictions rather than business benefits. The hallmark of the BA practice is a focus on value-based decision making.

RELIEVE THE BURDEN OF ANALYSIS

Why is it that contemporary corporations and public entities continue to invest heavily in projects with only marginal results or, even worse, outright failure? Business analysis is *the* critical missing component of the strategy execution framework. Without it, a disturbing percentage of programs and supporting projects are not on point to execute strategies or are too complex to be successful. Enterprise business analysis is the linchpin for making sound investment decisions—the bridge between strategy and execution.

In the 21st century it is more important than ever for an organization's leadership team to establish a vision and set strategic goals to innovate and thus remain competitive. But the leadership team cannot execute the strategy alone. It is through a robust portfolio of projects that strategies are converted into valuable programs and projects. What keeps organizations from successfully valuing and managing their project portfolio? The arduous and time-consuming *burden of analysis* is the barrier to optimum strategy execution through programs and projects.

Business leaders are beginning to realize that the burden of analysis can be relieved through the energy and expertise of the enterprise/strategic BA. Business analysts working to support executives and project portfolio directors provide the enterprise analysis, business architecture, tools, processes, and actionable information that decision-makers need to make the best possible investments. Often, too little energy and analysis go into determining the opportunities an organization will pursue.

ENLIST A SMALL TEAM OF EXPERTS

BAs lead the effort to delve deeper into the purpose of a new initiative, to describe in detail the opportunity to pursue or problem to solve—and why it is important. Determining the purpose of a new initiative is perhaps the first and most important step in the strategy execution process. It is at this point that you could pursue "business as usual" initiatives, solve the wrong problem, or, instead, foster the creativity and innovation that is needed for business success in today's economy.

Enterprise BAs start their work by using an array of analysis techniques to understand the current situation: competitive analysis, benchmark analysis, technology analysis, environmental analysis, organizational capability analysis, and market analysis. Armed with the results of these studies, they begin to determine the best path forward to execute strategy by working with a small expert team, resulting in the proposal for a new initiative.

THINK CREATIVELY

It is the expert team facilitated by an enterprise BA that decomposes the strategic goals that are not being addressed into achievable objectives that can be measured in terms of business benefits. The objectives are further decomposed into business problems to be solved or opportunities to be pursued to meet the objectives.

As discussed in Chapter 8, the enterprise BA uses creative idea-generating and problem-solving techniques to identify the most innovative opportunities to pursue. Recognizing that there is no shortage of problems to solve and opportunities to pursue, the team needs to take the time to select the most promising, valuable, and innovative initiatives. The BA instills the understanding that it is our responsibility to spend enough time and energy to truly understand the business, to conduct research and analysis of the opportunity, and to collaboratively "create" rather than simply "meet business needs."

THINK STRATEGICALLY

Once the most feasible solution idea is identified, the BA guides the team to consider the opportunity in its wider context. How will the opportunity offer value to customers more effectively and efficiently? How does the opportunity fit into the organization's overall strategy? How does it support an existing competitive advantage or create a new one? How does it support existing markets or create new ones? Thinking strategically involves examining the breadth of the opportunity:

- Describe the problem you are trying to solve or the opportunity you are considering in as much detail as possible. What makes this opportunity important? Who cares about it?

- Describe the big picture, the context in which the opportunity will operate.

- Identify the business strategy the proposed opportunity supports and determine how the proposed solution will promote this strategy.

- Determine how the opportunity aligns with the organization's vision, mission, operating model, guiding principles, goals, and targets.

- Be aware of how other projects contribute to business strategies to avoid duplication of efforts or interdependencies with other initiatives.

- Determine how the proposed project will sustain, enhance, or disrupt the organization's competitive advantage.

- Determine ways to link the opportunity to the key business measures that are used to describe the health of the business.

- Examine the potential value added to your customers and wealth to your organization.

EXAMINE THE "FIT" OF THE OPPORTUNITY

The team then examines the idea in more depth, beginning by determining if it has been tried in the past, either by your organization or one of your partners or competitors. If so, was it successful? If not, why not? Will the opportunity result in a creative, innovative new approach? Does this new opportunity fall logically within an existing line of business? Will it involve creating a new entity? What impacts will the opportunity have on:

- Current commercial practices

- Cultural norms and taboos

- Organizational policies and procedures

- Organizational structures and reporting relationships

- Current skills and competencies?

The opportunity analysis and innovation processes are forever joined. BAs champion the transition from a tactical to a strategic focus, which results in a compelling proposal that identifies the outcome to be achieved linked to strategies, value/business benefit projections, and the associated investment.

IDENTIFY THE BUSINESS SPONSOR

Business sponsors provide the financial resources for a project, dedicate business representatives to participate in the project, and are accountable for the business benefits expected from project outcomes. Before spending too much energy and expertise completing all the steps to analyze an opportunity and solution options, it is wise to make sure there is a sponsor for the effort. If not, the opportunity may not be worth pursuing. If that is the case, re-examine the situation to determine the best course of action.

A View from on the Ground

PROJECT BUSINESS MANAGER

Michele Maritato
Project Manager, Business Analyst Consultant

I helped one of my clients design the new company role of "project business manager" (PBM). A PBM is a professional who interacts at the very beginning directly with the customer to help in selecting the right project, thereby executing the BA role of enterprise analyst. Once the business case is approved, the PBM manages the project to achieve the objectives; the project manager is responsible for carrying out the project. When the project is completed, the PBM evaluates the new solution in terms of customer needs and suggests improvements to the solution to maximize the return on the investment forecast in the business case.

LEAD PROJECTS COLLABORATIVELY

BAs can employ several strategies to change the way we lead complex projects. Transition to a shared leadership approach and make sure you have seasoned leadership that is comfortable with complexity and uncertainty.

ESTABLISH SHARED LEADERSHIP

Traditionally, the project manager has been the project leader. Today's world of complexity, however, demands a shared approach to project leadership (see Figure 9-1). The leadership group comprises a core cluster of experts involved in project execution, typically the project manager, the enterprise business analyst, the business architect, the lead technologists (solution architect, lead developer, test manager), and the business visionary (not just a business representative, but a senior person who represents the project sponsor, has decision-making authority, and fully understands the organization's vision and strategies). The complex project leadership group is co-located, collaborates extensively, and shares leadership, each taking the lead when particular perspective, expertise, and talent are needed.

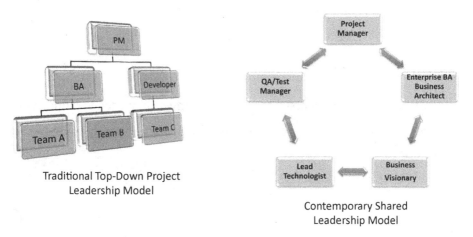

Traditional Top-Down Project
Leadership Model

Contemporary Shared
Leadership Model

FIGURE 9-1. Shared Leadership Model

USE COMPLEXITY THINKING TO MAKE PROJECT LEADERSHIP ASSIGNMENTS

The high failure rate of complex business projects is due in large part to two gaps in capabilities:

- Complex project managers

- Enterprise business analysts.

When dealing with complexity, ensure that your leadership is credible, influential, seasoned, and expert in both technical expertise and leadership. If there are gaps in the level of experience and knowledge, business benefits will erode. We don't always have control over our project resources—but we can examine the skills and experience of those in key roles and figure out how to close the gaps in needed expertise. Some strategies to close the expertise gaps include:

- Recruiting a mentor for the project leadership team from among the top performers in your organization

- Bringing in consultants or contractors with specific skills

- Focusing on managing risks and complexities.

MANAGE COMPLEXITY

For BAs to become successful leaders of change, they need to understand how to manage IT complexity and how to leverage it to bring about innovation.

THE REALITY OF IT COMPLEXITY

BAs like to say that they are engaged in business projects, not IT projects. However, information has become the life blood of businesses in every industry. Virtually every significant business process is supported by complex technology. Unfortunately, across the globe, we are losing billions of dollars per month on unsuccessful IT projects. The proliferation of IT project failures, coupled with the immense cost of maintaining large, complex IT systems, is eroding profits and draining resources. The opportunity for BA professionals is first to understand the magnitude of the problem of spiraling IT project failures and then to collaborate with other project professionals to turn the tide.

Complexity is increasing in IT systems as a result of the increase in interdependencies and interrelationships between functions within the system as well as the number of interfaces between systems. The more functions performed by the system, the higher the level of complexity and the more costly the system is to develop and maintain.

The way out of this situation is to eliminate, or significantly reduce, system interdependencies—to simplify. Simplification starts with system requirements and design. To begin to blur the line between requirements and design, the BA needs to work very closely with the solution architect. Decompose the system into a subset of business functions. Draft early requirements and designs for each function iteratively. As the requirements evolve for each function, the solution design emerges in iterations, with each iteration seeking to simplify the system. The requirements mirror the system design. The goal is to reduce interdependencies between solution functions and to minimize the connections to other systems.

ADAPTIVE, ITERATIVE METHODS

An understanding of complexity demands more adaptive approaches to managing projects. Even though project complexity is increasing, most projects still use linear paradigms to manage their projects. More iterative, adaptive models are needed to react to the unpredictable dynamics of the complex environment (see Figure 9-2). Just as requirements and designs are modular, construction, test, and delivery are also performed in iterations.

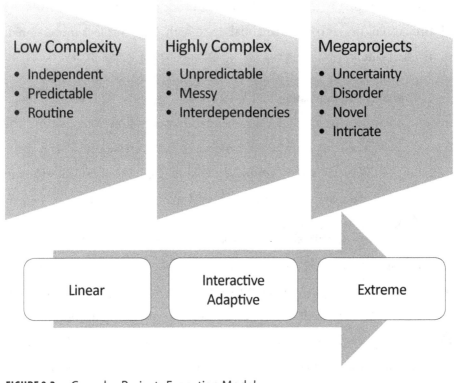

Low Complexity
- Independent
- Predictable
- Routine

Highly Complex
- Unpredictable
- Messy
- Interdependencies

Megaprojects
- Uncertainty
- Disorder
- Novel
- Intricate

Linear

Interactive Adaptive

Extreme

FIGURE 9-2. Complex Projects Execution Models

LOW COMPLEXITY PROJECTS

Linear models are typically effective for low complexity projects that are independent, i.e. there are no interrelationships that add complexity and uncertainty. The most commonly used linear approach is the waterfall model.

Linear methods work if dealing with well-understood maintenance, enhancement, and continuous-improvement projects when:

- The business problem, opportunity, and solution are clear

- Requirements are well understood

- No major changes are expected

- The organization has successfully done this before.

HIGHLY COMPLEX PROJECTS

When complexity creeps in because multiple interdependencies make it difficult to predict the behavior of the systems, more adaptive methods are needed. For iterative, adaptive methods, the large batches of work are decomposed into a series of small, timeboxed iterations. These smaller batches accelerate feedback and provide benefits that include easier mid-course correction, higher quality, greater release frequency, and better IT/business alignment. Because the interdependencies between functions are reduced, the cost of change is reduced.

Iterative, adaptive methods work because 21st century projects are often chaotic, unpredictable, and dynamic. Combining the elements of classical PM practices, agile methods, and lean product development generally yields far superior results.

MEGA PROJECTS

For mega projects where innovative methods and solutions are involved, overrun schedules and budgets are the name of the game; these call for extreme measures characterized by:

- Scaled-up agile practices

- Minimal early requirements

- Emergent architecture (many short experimental iterations to determine goals and identify the most viable solution)

- Customer involvement until the solution emerges:
  - o Terminates after the solution is found, or
  - o When the sponsor is unwilling to fund any more research.

MAXIMIZE BUSINESS VALUE

Sometimes business value is not realized because the complex new business solution is not deployed and operated effectively. Another area of our project culture that is in need of improvement is the transition process: transitioning to a new way of doing business when significant changes to products, services, or business practices are deployed.

Although business analysts are responsible for several types of requirements (e.g, business, stakeholder, solution), transition requirements are often inadequate (sometimes consisting of only training plans) or even nonexistent. Transition requirements should be laid out in documents and schematics describing how the business will operate when the solution is deployed, including changed/new processes, policies, business rules, roles, skills, tools, training plans, and potentially new business units.

Once transition requirements have been discovered, the BA works with the PM and other members of the core leadership team to develop a transition plan and schedule to meet all transition requirements, identify and manage risks and issues, and manage the transition. In addition, the transition plan takes into account the business value expected from the solution and ensures that value measurement systems are in place as an essential part of the new/changed solution.

After the solution is deployed, the BA monitors performance of the system and measures the benefits the organization has realized. The BA continues to change and improve the new solution to maximize value to customers and benefits to the organization's bottom line.

A View from on the Ground

GREAT BUSINESS ANALYSTS

Kate Gwynne
Associate Director, Business Analysis
Advertising Industry

Many project teams consider the end of a project to be when the new solution is launched. For an application or website, a project team deploys the software to production, handles maintenance items, and then they're off to start the next project. If they would go beyond just launching a solution and instead help their client understand how to implement and sustain that new product, they would become a strategic partner to their client.

Experienced BAs have the skills to help organizations implement solutions effectively by determining the people, processes, and tools impacted; addressing any risks, issues, and constraints that might be experienced; and determining if the solution has met the original project objectives. For this reason, BAs are natural change leaders in an organization.

PUTTING IT ALL TOGETHER

WHAT DOES THIS MEAN FOR THE BUSINESS ANALYST?

Strive to change the way you execute your BA practices, focusing on these important areas:

- Value-based decision-making

- Relieving the burden of analysis to select the most valuable projects

- Leading projects collaboratively to ensure that all needs are satisfied

- Managing complexity to reduce project failures

- Maximizing business value after the solution is deployed.

WHAT DOES THIS MEAN FOR THE BA MANAGER/PRACTICE LEAD?

Mature organizations devote significant time and energy to experimentation, trial and error, prototyping, and other creative endeavors before rushing to build new solutions. These research and analysis activities include enterprise analysis, competitive analysis, problem analysis, and creative-solution alternative analysis, all performed while exploring opportunities and selecting and prioritizing projects.

This value-based approach involves a significant cultural shift for most organizations—spending more time up front to make certain the proposed solution is creative and innovative. That solution can be introduced incrementally to manage complexity and elicit changes that add value.

If you are a BA practice lead, insist on up-front analysis before a business case is created and used to propose a new initiative. Begin to transition to iterative, adaptive requirements, design, and project management methods to manage complexity.

In Chapter 10, we focus on communicating strategically, which is a critical skill for BAs and BA manager/practice leads as they become credible leaders of change.

CHAPTER 10
Communicating Strategically

S trategic communication is not like your typical business communication—often a status update in the form of a one-page slide cluttered with information. Keep in mind that your communication is typically delivered to an information-overload sponsor or steering committee. Your communication needs to be concise, targeted, and always focused on business value as perceived by the audience.

Project sponsors seldom receive reports of business benefits from project outcomes that are measured accurately. The BA is responsible for communicating the expected—and then the actual—value derived from project and program solutions. The BA practice manager/lead is responsible for communicating the value of the solutions delivered through the project portfolio and the added value of business analysis practices. In addition, the BA lead ensures that these data are captured and disseminated far and wide—showcasing the business value of the BA practice.

For the BA practice lead who wants to be taken seriously as a credible leader of change, strategic communication is almost a silver bullet. In fact, it is vital for all BAs. Communicating strategically involves:

- Thinking holistically

- Crafting powerful messages

- Drafting a strategic communication plan

- Influencing positive decision-making.

THINKING HOLISTICALLY

The BA practice lead understands that the BA team is leading projects that are making changes to a set of parts connected by a web of relationships. Through these projects, the team is instrumental in executing strategy through multiple, interrelated changes. This is the story that needs to be told through strategic communications coming from BAs and especially from the BA practice lead, who are constantly participating in:

- *Strategy formation* through enterprise analysis, competitive analysis, and creative thinking

- *Strategy decomposition* to goals and objectives captured in the business case

- *Strategy execution* through programs and projects

- *Strategy correction/refinement* as more is learned and the environment changes

- *Strategy measurement* of progress along the journey

- *Strategy communication* that describes the progress and demonstrates business benefits realized through projects.

To elevate your messages and make sure they are heard, begin to think differently about projects. Engage in holistic thinking so that your view of project work is broad, comprehensive, and value-oriented. For example, holistic thinking brings about an understanding that:

- Projects are essential to the growth and survival of organizations

- Through projects we innovate and adapt to changes in the environment, the competition, and the marketplace

- Projects and project teams are our most effective tools for executing strategy and thereby creating value

- Strategic thinking transforms our perception of project teams from tactical implementers to strategic executers of change.

HOLISTIC THINKING

Holistic thinking, sometimes referred to as *systems thinking*, is the process of understanding the complexity of how systems influence one another within a whole. In nature this approach applies to how ecosystems such as air, water, movement, plants, and animals work together to survive or perish. In the context of business solutions, it is the study the relationships between elements of the business with each other and with other systems. Holistic thinking forms the basis for everything BA practice leads and enterprise BAs do:

- Examining a complex system

- Developing the business design structure (the business model)

- Solving problems

- Forming and executing strategy

- Managing change

- Managing communications.

In organizations, systems consist of people, structures, data, processes, and technology that work together to make an organization functional, dysfunctional, or somewhere in between. The only way to determine why a problem or opportunity exists is to examine it in relation to all the elements within its system.

ANALYTICAL THINKING

Holistic thinking needs to complement analytical thinking. Analytical thinking involves understanding a system by thinking about its parts and how they work together to produce larger-scale effects. We typically think that BAs engage exclusively in analytical thinking. However, BAs must employ holistic thinking as well to see the whole—all aspects of the business undergoing change.

- Holistic, systems thinkers get a general feeling about a situation to open their minds to subtle nuances of complex situations. They are often parallel processors, examining widespread simultaneous activity instead of a controlled, step-by-step process. They are creative and intuitive, focusing on the big picture and innovation.

- Analytical thinkers understand how the components of the system function and work together. They usually have good memories and pay close attention to the inner details of a situation.

BAs need to understand the difference between the holistic and analytical thinking, and when to employ each.

CRAFTING POWERFUL MESSAGES

When presenting information to overworked executives, managers, employees, and distracted customers, you have only a few minutes to get your message across. You need to become expert in constructing memorable messages, customizing your message for the audience, really getting your message heard, and getting the decisions you want quickly so that progress does not stall. For messages to be impactful and memorable, they must be targeted. And we need to be able to communicate our messages quickly.

THE ELEVATOR SPEECH

An elevator speech is a short statement used to quickly and simply define a person, project, product, service, organization, or event and its value. BAs need to know how to create it, rehearse it, and tailor it.

An effective elevator speech contains these elements:

- *Brevity.* Get your message across in no longer than 60 seconds.

- *Clarity.* Use clear, basic language. If you use elaborate verbiage to impress, you will likely lose your listener before your time is up.

- *Authoritative.* Use words that are compelling and durable.

- *Visual.* Create a vivid image in your listener's mind.

- *Story.* Convey a compelling message that tells a story by creating a captivating image of the message.

- *Targeted.* Target your message to a specific audience. If you have different target audiences, have a unique pitch for each.

- *Outcome-oriented.* Design your message with a specific outcome in mind. You may need different outcomes from different stakeholders

- *Enticing.* Leave your audience wanting more. Use a compelling "hook" that motivates people to engage further.

Write the first draft of the message in several different ways that capture your objectives. The goal is to get at many ideas as possible down on paper; leave the editing for later. It often helps to write a very short story that illustrates what you do for people. Create an image with words. Highlight the phrases that hook you. Rewrite to include the best words and phrases. Be ready to provide more detail by anticipating questions and responses. End by asking for something to continue the dialogue, such as a meeting or a lunch date.

Capture your building blocks and elevator speech for each stakeholder in a simple tabular template such as the one presented in Figure 10-1. Use this information to continually update and improve your message—keep it fresh! Practice delivering your elevator speech for each unique listener.

Stakeholder	Role in Project	WIIFM What's in it for me?	Influence Strategies	The Message	Catch Phrases	Slogan	Elevator Pitch/ Speech
Stakeholder #1							
Stakeholder #2							
Stakeholder #3							

FIGURE 10-1. Developing Custom Messages

MEMORABLE MESSAGES

Armed with the "business intelligence" you have captured and the political management plan you have developed (discussed in Chapter 2), you are ready to craft customized messages to your key stakeholders. This may be one of your most fruitful endeavors.

First, determine the purpose of the message. Is it simply to create awareness about your BA practice objectives? Is it to enlist support for your BA practice? Is it to dispel negative feelings about your BA practice? Is it to make a decision about your BA practice approach? Is it to gain support to resolve an issue? Is it to take a different approach to your project? Is it to communicate that the business case for a project is no longer valid?

Once you have zeroed in on the core purpose of the communication, draft the message, composing it from the stakeholder's perspective. Be sure to determine w*hat's in it for them* and tailor the message accordingly. Use familiar sales techniques to capture the attention of your audience and ensure that the message is remembered, like catch phrases and slogans that deftly capture the essence of what you are trying to say. The goal is for the catch phrase or slogan to capture the heart of your message in a snippet that the audience will remember.

For your message to hit the mark, you need to know what your target audience cares about: *What's in it for me?*

WHAT'S IN IT FOR THE CIO?

CIOs are well aware that many of their very costly IT-intensive projects, whether for technology infrastructure upgrades, improved business capabilities, or a new product or service, fail to achieve expected value. Furthermore, they are frustrated and unclear about how to fix the problem.

If business analysis practices produce convincing business cases and value-based measurement techniques, CIOs will be able to predict, deliver, and demonstrate real value. BAs need to produce believable business cases and then accurately measure results.

Your message to your CIO might be: *"Enlightened CIOs are placing their bets on world class business analysis to be able to empower innovation and realize real business value from IT."*

WHAT'S IN IT FOR THE BUSINESS MANAGER?

Executives often put a mid- to senior-level manager in charge of expensive project investments for a department or line of business. So not only is the CIO being held accountable for driving value to the customer and wealth to the bottom line, but front-line management is also on the hook.

This might be your message to your business manager: *"When you need to get it right, enterprise and solution analysis will invest in innovative solutions and deliver real value through projects."*

WHAT'S IN IT FOR THE TECHNOLOGIST?

Similarly, CIOs put a mid- to senior-level IT manager in charge of the technology for expensive IT project investments. So not only is the CIO being held accountable for driving value to the customer and wealth to the bottom line, but front-line IT management is also on the hook. Assuming the business analyst partners with the business manager and lead technologist who are on point when creating the business cases, they will be invaluable in helping keep the focus on the business benefits.

Your message to your lead technologist might be something like: *"An experienced BA assigned throughout the project increases your probability of success by a whopping 400 percent."*

WHAT'S IN IT FOR THE PROJECT MANAGER?

Whether or not there is a convincing business case, the PM is expected to deliver the solution on time and on budget. The PM cares about cost—but project cost as opposed to the total cost of ownership of the new solution. PMs generally don't focus on the cost to operate or maintain the new solution, only on the build or acquisition costs. As a result, project success to PMs is often determined by measures other than business value.

The business analyst keeps the focus on the business value expected from the new solution, collaborating with the PM to conduct trade-off analysis and make the tough project decisions. The business analyst also has an ear to the ground to determine if business needs are changing that might affect the current project objectives.

Your message to your PM might be something like this: *"A PM increases the probability of project success by a whopping 400 percent with an exceptional BA on the project."*

DRAFTING A STRATEGIC COMMUNICATION PLAN

In this chaotic world of content coming at us in all directions, a systematic approach to communication will return huge dividends. A strategic communication plan will help you gain and sustain support for your BA practice and increase your credibility and status in your organization. It will ensure that you provide consistent information to all key supporters and stakeholders.

Communication is strategic when it is completely consistent with your mission, vision, and values and is able to enhance the standing of your BA practice in the organization. It helps you focus your objectives, profile your target audience, identify the appropriate communication tools to reach your audience, implement the plan, and manage and measure your results.

Creating a strategic communication plan is likely a cultural shift for your organization. You are transforming the way you do projects; transforming your communication approaches is a critical success factor. Indeed, your communication plan "sells" your BA practice or your project to those whose support you need.

Be sure to start communication from the top and then radiate it down through the entire organization. Use your executive sponsor and steering committee to approve your communication approach and to get the word out. Your communication plan should take into account stakeholder needs and should also include more detailed information if more background is needed during follow-up discussions. Consider using multiple channels, including online search, social, and digital, if your company is using these methods. The plan highlights the timing and media used as well as who on your team is the lead for each stakeholder or group.

INFLUENCING POSITIVE DECISION-MAKING

Another opportunity to use strategic communication is when presenting recommendations to decision-makers. If you need a decision—most likely from your executive sponsor or steering committee—include decision support information about the need, the problem, all options considered, and the team's recommendation. Executives are busy people; they need to see that you understand the problem/opportunity and have reviewed all options available. In short, you need to steer your steering committee.

Many BA practice implementations are challenged—or even fail—because the BA practice lead does not perform the critical analysis needed to determine the best path forward, not only at the start of the BA practice, but also along the way as more is learned and issues arise. The BA practice lead too often does not take the time to analyze all possible solutions to problems and to assess varying approaches before marching ahead.

Once you are clear about the problem or opportunity the BA practice will address, there are still so many questions: Should we resource the practice in house? Do we have the appropriately skilled and talented BAs? Are they available? Do we need outside expertise? How fast do we need the practice to be fully functional? What are our competitors doing? The list goes on and on. This is also true of your BAs who are working on critical projects. They often do not take a step back and really think through recommendations. Don't go to a decision-making meeting without first doing your homework.

GETTING THE DECISION YOU WANT

When proposing a new initiative, escalating issues, proposing a course correction, securing the best resources for your practice/project, or advocating for scope changes that add business value, you are essentially in a sales role, seeking approval from upper management. Your message must be clear, concise, and compelling. You must not only be brief, but you must also demonstrate the wisdom of the recommendation you are making. Work with an expert team to conduct problem/alternative analysis.

USING PROBLEM/ALTERNATIVE ANALYSIS

So, how can you make sure you get the decision you want? You need to involve your team and perhaps some of your steering committee members, augmenting them with SMEs who are influential and knowledgeable about the situation at hand, to analyze the issues, identify all potential options, and propose the most feasible solution. Use the results of your alternative analysis as decision-support information when presenting your recommended approach. Include the names of those who participated in the analysis, all the options considered, and the feasibility of each option: economic feasibility, time-to-market feasibility, cultural feasibility, technical feasibility, success feasibility, business process feasibility, and the feasibility of achieving an innovative solution.

Once this analysis is complete, it becomes clear which option is the most feasible. Capture your feasibility analysis in a simple Alternative Analysis Worksheet (see Figure 10-2) and use it as decision support information when meeting with your sponsor or steering committee.

Problem, Opportunity, or Issue
Expert Team Members Involved in Analysis

Option	Cost Economic Feasibility	Benefits Success Feasibility	Innovative	Time Feasibility	Cultural Feasibility	Probability of Success	Process Complexity	Technical Complexity	Risks
Option #1									
Option #2									
Option #3									
Option #4									
Option #5									

FIGURE 10-2. Alternative Analysis Worksheet

PUTTING IT ALL TOGETHER

WHAT DOES THIS MEAN FOR THE BUSINESS ANALYST?

Create a strategic communication plan to manage stakeholders' influence, develop your communication skills, respond to political risks, and seek approval for recommendations that are supported by rigorous alternative and feasibility analysis. Your team will respect you, and your management team will notice your logical and disciplined approach.

WHAT DOES THIS MEAN FOR THE BA MANAGER/PRACTICE LEAD?

To communicate effectively, the BA practice lead prepares unique communication strategies for each major stakeholder. Your goal is to explain the value of business analysis, driving an understanding of WIIFM ("What's in it for me?") for all key stakeholders. Effective communication involves an enterprise focus—an emphasis on executing strategy and advancing enterprise capabilities, delivering innovative products and services, and measuring and communicating improved project outcomes and solution value.

Include the appropriate media and timing of the communication in your plan. After each communication, determine the effectiveness of the message and make improvements for the next time. Require your BAs to employ these proven communication techniques as they negotiate the political landscape.

In Chapter 11 we turn to the need for BAs and the BA manager/practice lead to demonstrate exceptional leadership and turn a strong team into a high-performing team.

CHAPTER 11
Leading Your High-Performing Team

Business leaders have responsibility for developing and sustaining teams as well as for ensuring that the individual and collective efforts of team members are directed toward creating value and executing strategy. Team leadership is more a role than a title or a position. The BA practice lead and the BA practitioners contribute to developing and maintaining cohesive teams that perform at their highest potential.

High-performing teams are essential for your organization to respond to the competitive pressures in ever-changing domestic and global markets. BAs live and breathe as key team leaders and members in many team configurations, including project teams, virtual teams, product development teams, and autonomous work teams.

In Chapter 4 we focused on building a capable BA workforce able to control and leverage complexity. We now turn to the need for the BA practice lead (and individual BAs as well) to become an exceptional team leader. Strong teams have strong leaders. Just like a professional coach, the BA practice lead's job is all about building and sustaining a high-performing team—your BA team and the project teams your BAs support. Fielding a *great* BA team requires more than just BA capability. High performance depends on superior team leadership and enlightened, passionate team members.

HIGH-PERFORMING TEAMS

Examples of high-performing teams are all around us: emergency responders, symphony orchestras, and professional sports teams. These teams demonstrate their prowess, creativity, accomplishments, insights, and enthusiasm daily and are a testament to the power of teams. Yet the business project environment, especially the IT project environment, has been slow to make the most of the power of teams. The BA practice team is uniquely positioned to unleash this great power and drastically improve project performance.

To understand how to take your team from a capable group of BAs to a remarkable and celebrated team of BAs, use high-performing teams as a model. When you think of great teams you have observed, which teams come to mind? High-performing teams are the product of leadership, urgency, focus, and discipline.

PARAMEDIC TEAMS

Paramedic teams mean the difference between surviving and succumbing to an overwhelming health emergency. Paramedics consistently provide medical care at an advanced life support level, usually in an emergency, at the location of an onset of illness or injury. Paramedics almost always work in teams of two to four specialists. Each fully understands his/her role and how it integrates into the whole approach to assess the degrees of urgency to wounds or illnesses and to provide life-saving interventions. It is about expertise, the importance of the mission, clear roles, and team resolve.

FIREFIGHTING TEAMS

A New York City firefighter who had been with his squad for decades explained how he handled such a pressure-filled job by saying: "I would pay them to let me be a firefighter." He was talking about the camaraderie, the team spirit, the brotherhood, and the importance of the mission.

SYMPHONY ORCHESTRAS

The Boston Symphony Orchestra, Inc. (BSO) presents more than 250 concerts annually. It is an ensemble that has richly fulfilled its vision of a great and permanent orchestra in Boston. BSO has been the scene of almost 200 American premieres over the last century. It's about expertise, cultural and historical contributions, and first-rate group performances.

HEART TRANSPLANT/OPERATING ROOM TEAMS

Transplant patient survival depends on well-orchestrated care delivered by the transplant team. Many historic transplants have been achieved by a team of physicians, surgeons, and researchers. It's about top-of-their-game performance; superior medicine; highly skilled, interdisciplinary teams; and progressive, innovative techniques and technology.

NAVY SEALS

And then there are the Navy Seals, perhaps the most famous of all great teams. Seal Team Six (ST6) is a multifunctional special operations unit with several roles that include high-risk specialized missions. Required entrance skills include combat experience, language skills, and the ability to blend in as civilians during an operation. Members are selected in part because of the diversity of skills of each team member. The ST6 training schedule is without comparison in its intensity. ST6 is renowned for its amazing accomplishments.

NEW PRODUCT DEVELOPMENT/INNOVATION TEAMS

Business success stories based on the strategic use of teams for new product development are plentiful. Apple is at the top of nearly everyone's list when it comes to innovation. For Apple it's about innovation, creating things we don't even know we want or need.

3M relies on teams to develop its new products. These teams are cross-functional, collaborative, autonomous, and self-organizing. The teams deal well with ambiguity, accept change, take initiative, and assume risks.

Toyota continues to boast the fastest product development times in the automotive industry, is a consistent leader in quality, has a wide variety of products designed by a lean engineering staff, and has consistently grown its U.S. market share.

HIGH-PERFORMANCE TEAM LEADERSHIP IN THE WORLD OF BUSINESS ANALYSIS

What makes some teams effective and others extraordinary—and how can we build and sustain high-performing teams in our BA world?

To build and lead an extraordinary practice team of BAs, we need to know what all great teams have in common. Pick your favorite team as a model for your BA practice. Pay close attention. Essentially all effective team leaders use certain key strategies. Work to get your team to embrace these principles, to live them. Discuss them, devise mechanisms to reinforce them, and model them during every interaction with your team. When these elements are compromised, team performance suffers; when they come together, it is magic.

BAs and BA leads need to understand the importance of these team characteristics and simulate them to build their team leadership prowess:

- *Vision/mission-focused.* Great teams understand the strategic criticality of their efforts, the mission, and the value of their work. They have a common set of values and guiding principles. They are passionate about the mission, the work, and the results. Reinforce the mission of business analysis at every opportunity: creating value to customers and wealth to the bottom line.

- *Small but mighty.* Keep your team of BAs small. If the team is too big, members lose their sense of camaraderie and purpose. People begin to look at your group as a cost rather than a strategic cluster of experts who add real value. Foster a team mindset. The solidarity of teams makes us part of something bigger than ourselves.

- *Full-time, co-located, shared leadership.* An important tenet of high-performing teams is co-location. Each day begins with a short meeting to bring everyone up to speed on happenings, problems, and priorities. The team gathers to review the status of each major project. Establish a quick round-the-horn quality to the meetings. This addresses the most important issues quickly. If co-location is out of the question, hold these meetings using cutting-edge virtual collaboration tools.

- *Highly trained and highly practiced.* All great teams continually hone their skills. And then they practice, practice, practice! As BA practice lead, send your BAs to conferences and training sessions on advanced techniques, industry innovations, and technical trends. Insist that they report back to the whole group on what they have learned. Plan lots of time for training, practice, feedback, improvement, and more practice.

- *Diverse, multi-skilled.* A high-performing team needs a variety of skills, capabilities, talents, and dexterity to understand all the perspectives of complex situations. Constantly review the diversity of your team members—diversity of expertise, seniority levels, even age and gender. Diversity facilitates gathering a broad array of perspectives and ideas before decisions are made.

- *Experienced.* There is simply no substitute for experience. Get the right mix of seasoned, up-and-coming, and relatively new BAs. Seasoned BAs bring solid expertise; new BAs bring energy, motivation, excitement, and ease with the latest technologies.

- *Personally accountable.* Each member of your team needs to hold him/herself personally responsible and accountable for the success of the mission. The mission—to add value to your customers and wealth to your bottom line—needs to be in the forefront of every team member's psyche.

- *Expertly coached.* Behind all great teams is an inspiring, loyal coach who consistently removes barriers to the team's success. As BA practice lead, take extraordinary care of your team. Your team members are your most important asset.

- *Creative.* Creativity is as much a matter of mindset and technique as it is intelligence. Give your team permission to be creative and the skills and techniques to pull it off. Conduct sessions with your team members to help them understand creativity and foster innovation.

- *Holistic, systems thinkers.* Great teams see the whole picture and understand how complex teams need to adapt as the environment changes or more is learned. At every opportunity, relate day-to-day activities to the strategy and core values of your organization and the mission of your BA practice. During daily meetings, ensure that the team considers the big picture before making decisions to solve problems.

- *Keep score.* Be sure to keep score and constantly improve your methods, approaches, relationships, quality, training, communications, and therefore, results.

LEAD YOUR TEAM TO DISTINCTION

Virtually all work today is accomplished by teams of people. Sometimes there are even teams of teams comprising groups from around the globe. We as BA leaders need to develop our team leadership skills fast. The BA practice has only a short time to make a good first impression.

Team leadership is different from traditional management, and teams are different from operational work groups. When leading high-performing, creative teams, it is no longer about command and control; rather, it is about collaboration, consensus, empowerment, confidence, and inspiration. It's not about operational efficiency; it's about innovation and value. Complex project teams are challenged today because of people failing to come together with a common vision, an understanding of complexity and creativity, and the right expertise.

The team leader's challenge is to leverage the synergy within the group so that the team process produces results that individuals working alone would not be capable of accomplishing. Explore leadership models that share the leadership role within the team. Develop a real understanding of each team member's strengths and passions. Insist on mutual accountability within the team and create an environment that is transparent and fun and that promotes healthy and spirited discussion.

ADJUST YOUR LEADERSHIP STYLE BASED ON TEAM NEEDS

Your personal motivation and interaction style will influence team performance. Steer and guide your team through the evolutionary phases of team development. Understand that teams go through stages and adjust your leadership style accordingly.

To develop and sustain high performance, it is helpful to understand the key stages of team development. Bruce Tuckman's classic team development model has become an accepted standard for how teams develop (see Figure 11-1 and Table 11-1). Become well acquainted with this model to understand how team needs change based on the stages of team development.

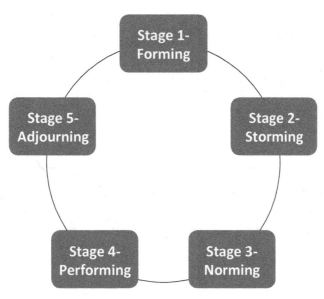

FIGURE 11-1. Tuckman Team Development Model

Team Characteristics	Forming	Storming	Norming	Performing
Team Leader Style	Directing, presenting objectives, scope, and process to be followed	Supportive, active listening, managing conflict, driving consensus	Collaborative, shared leadership	Coaching, removing barriers, empowering, motivating, getting out of the way
Team Member Behaviors	Tentative, slow to participate	Vying for position, conflict	Trust and respect for team members, support for leaders	Positive, professional, creative, highly effective
Team Process	Driven by the team leader	Not working well due to conflict	Operating smoothly	Well-functioning and adapting as necessary
Trust	Low level	Alliances forming	Trusting relationships forming	High levels of trust, loyalty, respect

Team Characteristics	Forming	Storming	Norming	Performing
Decision-Making	Leaders make decisions	Difficulty making decisions, members unwilling to compromise	Consensus decision-making	Decisions made quickly by consensus, some decisions are delegated to subgroups or individuals

TABLE 11-1. Team Characteristics in Tuckman Model Stages

Another quick view of team development, and the way team leaders adjust their leadership style is the Kolb model (see Table 11-2). It is particularly important for the BA lead to know when and how to assume a particular team leadership style as teams move in and out of development phases.

Kolb Team Development Stage	Team Leadership Mode
Building stage	Facilitator
Learning stage	Mediator
Trusting stage	Coach
Working stage	Consultant
Flowing stage	Collaborator

TABLE 11-2. Kolb Team Development Model

PROMOTE TEAM SUCCESS THROUGH YOUR INFLUENCE AND LEADERSHIP

Demonstrate a commitment to your people as well as to tasks and results. This is the first priority for team leaders. Get to know your team members and what makes them excited to come to work. Use tailored motivation and interaction styles to influence each team member's performance. Constantly conduct team health checks. Ask the team members to develop a checklist of team health areas to use as a self-assessment tool. Demonstrate to your team:

- Your priority to support and serve the team as well as to lead it

- Your enthusiasm, energy, inspiration, and expertise

- Your willingness to shoulder responsibility rather than pass the buck

- Your ability to make the team come together to achieve more than a group of individuals ever could.

JUMPSTART YOUR TEAM TO BUILD MOMENTUM

To create the infrastructure for high performance, the BA practice lead (and the BA lead on a project) needs to start the team off right. What are the mechanics of starting up and laying the foundation for a high performance team? The first and most important consideration is your team members.

GET THE RIGHT PEOPLE

The first step to high performance is getting the right people on your team. Conventional wisdom tells us that an organization needs to set an inspiring vision and well-developed strategy, and then to get people aligned behind the direction. Indeed, a common vision is essential for a team to gel and to elevate its behavior to high performance. The BA practice lead should consider several dynamics when recruiting, building, and taking care of a high-performance team:

- Get the people with the right BA capabilities (discussed in Chapter 4), accompanied by business/technology expertise and leadership prowess to lead 21st century complex initiatives

- Get the people who share your vision, passion, core values, accountability, and self-discipline

- Move the wrong people off your team

- Steer, guide, nurture, and lead your team to distinction.

Use complexity thinking to make decisions about building, leading, and developing your team. Again, as projects become more complex, more sophisticated leadership abilities are required. Do not compromise when getting the right people on your team because demand for BAs is outpacing your available BA resources. The goal is to end up with a team of BAs that are talented, passionate individuals who are a perfect fit for your organization based on its core values. The wrong people cannot be motivated to do the right thing; the right people cannot be stopped. The best hedge in an uncertain, complex world is making the right decision about who you have on your team. To build and sustain an enduring BA team, it must have a culture of people who are trusted, disciplined, fun, and who love to work hard.

GET A MIX OF EXPERTS AND NEW BLOOD

A healthy and enduring team has a mix of expert and seasoned members, sprinkled with less experienced but highly motivated individuals. Expertise is different from capability. Expertise is about knowhow, experience, and holistic thinking accompanied by the ability to view one's skill and knowledge in the larger context. Experts are not afraid of failure; they know failure is part of the innovation process. Experts respect the contributions of others, and welcome questions and challenges to their views. Experts love to mentor and coach young, new, energetic team members.

ESTABLISH A POSITIVE, CREATIVE, YET DISCIPLINED INFRASTRUCTURE

From day one, set the tone for the BA practice. Leadership is much more challenging today. BAs are faced with how radically things have changed and continue to change. Operating in a puzzling new atmosphere devoid of certainty, where the speed of change is unparalleled and the dynamics of interdependent issues are more complex than ever, many leaders are left feeling baffled.

This new world requires agility, the ability to adapt, and skills and instincts to react with speed and flexibility. Traditional leadership models are less reliable in this new world. Innovation and new ideas are vital, yet results are unpredictable. How can your team stay focused on immediate needs, yet continue to articulate a vision for transforming how your organization uses business analysis? How can you set a new team in motion that can make a difference—fast?

SET AND REINFORCE THE TONE

Combine business smarts with fun and a few flashes of inspiration. A creative team needs both direction and freedom—with a little excitement thrown in along the way. Provide direction for your team, but then get out of their way so team members are empowered to experiment, prototype, and test new ideas.

Pay special attention to the elements of all great teams. Discuss them with your team every chance you have. Collaborate with your team members to develop mechanisms to institutionalize the elements. Pick one to highlight for team development every time you have the whole team together. And have the whole team together often. Leverage the experts on your team.

Have them design and lead development sessions based on one of the aspects of great teams.

CAPITALIZE ON EARLY WINS

Every change expert advises new teams to take advantage of low-hanging fruit, to produce quick, easy wins. Engage your team to identify potential quick wins. Then, make sure everyone is aware of the difference you and your team are making. Use every opportunity to promote yourself and your team.

SUSTAIN HIGH PERFORMANCE TO MAKE LASTING CHANGE

How do you take your team of BAs from a *good* group to an impressive, remarkable, and celebrated team?

TAKE EXCEPTIONAL CARE OF YOUR TEAM

Assuming you have the right people on your team in terms of capabilities, and the team members believe in your core values and are passionate about your mission, the BA practice lead's job is to support them, develop them, and inspire them. Hold periodic offsite sessions to advance skills, reinforce your mission, reinforce the core values and elements of great teams, and build camaraderie. Recognize and celebrate the unique value of the individuals on your team.

Realize that high performance is intense. It is exhausting. Like a sprint, it is very difficult to sustain over long periods of time. Allow your team to rest and recover from episodes requiring intensity.

INSTILL CONFIDENCE IN YOUR BAS TO UNLEASH THEIR POWER AND INFLUENCE

The barriers to building BA influence skills can be both individual (self-inflicted) and organizational (caused by culture and management actions or inactions). Strategies to institutionalize the influence of your BAs include the following:

- Make business architecture artifacts relate to project requirements so everyone can see the big picture.

- Clarify the BA role so everyone knows it's about value and innovation; begin to call BAs *consultants* instead of *analysts*.

- Provide BAs with a framework for determining the importance of individual requirements based on value.

- Teach BAs to tailor their engagement style to the values and needs of their project sponsors and team members.

- Ensure that BAs engage early and often with both the business and technical teams.

- Encourage BAs to expand their toolkit to increase understanding of the business domain.

- Push BAs to become better challengers in conversations with business sponsors.[1]

DELIVER VALUE EARLY AND OFTEN

Be sure you build an infrastructure that can deliver real value often. Your projects need to do this—and so does your BA practice. Deliver value, measure the real value you have delivered, and communicate about it continually. Keep your eye on the business case to make sure you are on target to deliver the value that was predicted earlier, cheaper, better.

MAINTAIN INSPIRATION AND A CULTURE OF DISCIPLINE

It is a commonly held misconception that the imposition of standards and discipline discourages creativity. A project team is like a start-up company. To truly innovate, the team needs to value creativity, imagination, empowerment, and risk-taking. However, to maintain a sense of control over a large team, we often impose structure, insist on planning, and institutionalize coordination systems of meetings and reports.

The goal is to learn how to use rigor and discipline to *enable* creativity. Great teams (think emergency responders and surgical teams) almost always have rigid standards; they practice the execution of those standards over and over again until they become second nature. The team members work hard to examine each performance and improve the standards based upon experience.

LEVERAGE THE ADVANTAGES OF VIRTUAL TEAMS

While co-location is the ideal, a mobile, hyperconnected workforce has become the norm in the 21st century. Technology has made it easy to connect instantly with anyone all around the globe. Ensure that each virtual team embraces shared, co-located leadership. Exploit the benefits of global teams:

- Global teams afford us access to a broad array of talented team members with diverse skills and cultural prowess.

- Today's employees, especially the younger generation, want flexibility and are motivated by a culture that rewards accomplishments as opposed to time clocked in the office.

- Your attention will no longer be focused on structure, activities, and long workdays. Rather, you will focus on and look for results. This will free you and your team to become more strategic, building relationships and support for the team's efforts.

Of course, leaders of dispersed teams face unique challenges. Take action to minimize the added complexity of working with distributed teams. Learn new ways to manage. Remember that your influence can be more effective than your authority. Work to optimize your influence skills.

Integrating deliverables from different teams across cultures becomes difficult in a virtual team. Form integration teams to manage these risks and complexities. Recognize that distant team members may feel isolated and disconnected, so involve them as often as possible. Establish state-of-the-art knowledge-sharing approaches to keep all team members engaged.

PUTTING IT ALL TOGETHER

WHAT DOES THIS MEAN FOR THE BUSINESS ANALYST?

For BAs, continually learn about great teams and effective team leadership. Strive to collaborate with your other project leaders (PM, architect, lead developer, business visionary) to take your current project team from a good, capable group to a great, high-performing team.

WHAT DOES THIS MEAN FOR THE BA MANAGER/ PRACTICE LEAD?

For the BA practice lead, spend most of your time, effort, and passion on building a credible, respected team of BAs. Strive to make BAs a vital part of every critical change initiative in your organization. If you have a passionate, disciplined team of BAs, your job will be a delight!

Build a team that can stimulate creativity and innovation, adapt to market forces, and tap into other organizational resources to drive breakthrough results. Approach team building at the strategic level, targeting your BA resources to the most important projects. Learn about the structure, management, and dynamics of high-performing teams.

We conclude by considering the business analyst of the not-so-distant future, who will embrace organizational values, empower teams to succeed, bring customers into the change process, and drive innovation through global partnerships.

NOTES

1   Mark Tonsetic, "Do Your Business Analysts Lack Influence Power?" *CEB IT Quarterly*, Q1 2014, pp. 10–13.

Looking Ahead: BAs of the Future

BAs of the not-too-distant future (and their colleagues, PMs) must and will become visionaries, innovators, strategists, and transformational leaders, executing strategy through project results. Successful BAs will learn how to embrace organizational values, empower their teams to succeed, bring customers into the change process, and drive innovation through global partnerships. Don't miss out on these new ways of doing our work.

Business analysis has energizing new challenges and opportunities ahead. We need to change the way we do projects to achieve faster time to market and deliver innovative solutions that add value to the customer and wealth to the organization. Only then will we be contributing to a sustained competitive advantage for our organizations.

Many business analysis specialties and focus areas are needed in today's complex organizations. We examine just a few.

BA AS STRATEGIST

Strategic analysis is at the top of the food chain for BAs. Once you have established your credibility and influence, work to help develop and execute your organization's strategy. Strategy is an integrated, overarching concept of how the business will achieve its objectives. An organization's strategy answers these questions:

- Customers: who will we serve?

- Locations: where will we be active?

- Processes: how will we get there?

- Distinctions: how will we win in the marketplace?

- Timing: what will be our speed and sequence?

- Wealth: how will we realize our returns?

The strategic BA's role in strategy development is to relieve the burden of analysis from executives by knowing how to conduct these activities:

- Analyze problems

- Experiment

- Identify opportunities

- Determine business requirements

- Search for alternatives

- Evaluate solutions

- Conduct feasibility analysis

- Conduct business case analysis

- Perform benefits/value management

- Capitalize on complexity to bring about creativity.

BA AS BUSINESS PROCESS EXPERT

Many companies are committed to operational innovation through a focus on process management. These companies use sophisticated process management techniques to solve specific challenges at the cutting edge of process mastery. Virtually all important projects require some level of process change. BAs need to appreciate the role of process optimization in bringing about operational innovation.

BA AS ARCHITECT

Leading-edge businesses are embracing architectural techniques and beginning to "think visually" about the enterprise to reduce uncertainty and increase business agility. Enterprise business analysts fill an architectural role, integrating differing views of the enterprise to facilitate innovation through business blueprints that bring the organization alive and in focus.

Business architecture enables us to harness complexity and improve business outcomes by integrating strategy, operations, and IT into the whole to answer the questions:

> *How can your organization achieve sufficient business agility to accomplish your objectives among growing economic uncertainty? Does your business model take advantage of smarter technology and differentiating capabilities? Ultimately, are you capitalizing across business and IT to embrace increasing complexity to become a standout performer in your industry?*[1]

BA AS RULES/DECISION ANALYST

In this knowledge economy, your business is smart when it acts on the basis of rules, knows what its rules are, and can communicate those rules clearly. Business rules analysts help bring about consistency and order. The BA needs to understand, help build, interpret, use, and maintain an effective set of decision support rules and models. The University of Cambridge offers succinct definitions of the most commonly used decision support tools *(www.ifm.eng.cam.ac.uk/research/dstools/value-chain)*.

BA AS TECHNOLOGY-DRIVEN CHANGE EXPERT

A great source of knowledge about technology-driven change is Gartner, Inc., the information technology research and advisory company (*www.gartner.com*). To seize opportunities in this area, keep a close eye on trends in technology-driven change; Gartner offers the following suggestions to capitalize on current trends:

1. Build boundary-less teams and partners.

2. Help your company learn how to manage, monetize, operate, and extend the Internet as its product/service delivery system of choice.

3. Consider mobile apps a delivery strategy.

4. Help your business take ownership of process and intelligence to leverage "big data."

5. Reject preconceived data and technology limitations.

6. Explore innovative approaches for your company's products and services.

7. Rethink trust and identity in the fight against identity theft and cyber thievery.

8. Embrace web-scale IT.

9. Learn from the cloud and mobility movements.

10. Help your IT become an agile product and service provider to be truly innovative.[2]

BA AS BUSINESS/TECHNOLOGY OPTIMIZATION EXPERT

Opportunities abound for you to help your organization optimize its business/technology assets. The following are a few ideas:

1. Social technologies are changing the way we work, live, and play. Use these to reach your customers and employees. Change as social media changes so your organization remains on the leading edge.

2. Big data and advanced analytics present many areas of opportunity for BAs. Consider this a field you may want to explore.

3. Use the Internet in innovative ways to reach more and more customers.

4. Conduct creative sessions to identify opportunities to offer existing assets in new ways.

5. Help your company think globally to engage in emerging markets.

6. Merge the digital and physical components of your products by using clever apps such as wristband computers.

7. Embrace Internet-inspired personalization and simplification. Become expert at intuitive customer access to products and services.[3]

BA AS VALUE CREATOR

As we have emphasized repeatedly, it's all about business value—value to your customers and wealth to your bottom line. Focus on value in everything you do. If an activity is not adding value to your project, then don't do it.

BA AS AGILIST

Strive to become an agile BA. Agile, incremental projects are taking the world by storm because iteration is the best defense against complexity and risk. Smaller projects are simply easier to manage because fewer decisions must be made and fewer dependencies must be managed. So what does the BA do on an agile project? Again, the focus is on value:

- Value: Use value to prioritize work in backlog.

- Visualization: Use models, acceptance criteria, stories, and examples to describe what to build.

- Collaboration: Collaborate to determine what is "just enough." Remember, typically only 20 percent of features and functions are used.

- Brainstorming: Use divergent thinking (brainstorming) to create options and then convergent thinking (prioritizing, analyzing feasibility) to select the most valuable choices among the options.

- Analysis: Analyze when you need to, not before.

- Tools: Use tools to visualize what the work is and how it is progressing. Use integrated requirements management tools to store BA artifacts for reuse.

Barbara Carkenord, BA thought leader at RMC, offers sage advice about the agile BA. Iteration, Carkenord tells us, is effective because it:

- Uses release plans, where each release has a small, manageable scope

- Delivers products (and therefore, value) faster

- Allows developers to deliver software faster than we can analyze requirements

- Focuses on business value

- Fosters collaboration, teamwork, trust, and facilitation

- Uses simple techniques such as decision analysis, scope modeling, and user stories

- Rarely uses traditional requirements.

BA AS VIRTUAL TEAM LEADER

Global partnerships, alliances, and teams are an effective strategy to expand resources and to capture the nuanced requirements of different global markets. Indeed, about 80 percent of project teams today have members who are not physically co-located. Seeking partnerships and forming global teams are high-priority endeavors in this global economy.

Virtual teams add significant complexity to change initiatives. Use dispersed teams to expand your access to the talent you need. Innovation teams pose unique complexities that require sophisticated team leadership techniques. To succeed as a virtual BA lead, establish an environment of adaptability, flexibility, experimentation, and creativity. Applying the most appropriate practices, tools, technology, and techniques to multiple contributors, scattered in different locations across the globe, at the right time is in itself a complex endeavor. Successful virtual teams are the result of many elements coming together, including team structure, composition, culture, location, collaboration, communication, coordination, and evolution—and most of all, team leadership.

BA AS TRANSFORMATIONAL CHANGE AGENT

Incremental continuous improvements to the way we do things today are not enough in interconnected, innovation-driven economy of the 21st century. Transformational change is the call to action for BAs and BA managers/practice leads. Transformational change is very different from incremental change in that it is profound, fundamental, disruptive, and irreversible. It involves breakthrough practices, structures, business models, and technologies.

Examine current and future projects to assign the most seasoned BAs to transformational endeavors. Transformational change experts are skilled in these areas:

- Vision

- Holistic thinking

- Clear goals

- Understanding of the as-is current state, the to-be innovative future state, and the gap between them

- Sophisticated risk management and change management

- Complexity management

- Cultural change management.

A View from on the Ground

TRENDS IN BUSINESS ANALYSIS AND PROJECT MANAGEMENT

Andrea Brockmeier, PMP, Vicki James, PMP, CBAP, Elizabeth Larson, PMP, CBAP, CSM, and Richard Larson, PMP, CBAP
Watermark Learning, Inc.

It is helpful to reflect on what has occurred in business analysis and project management in the past and think about future trends. To summarize, the need for project managers and business analysts to be trusted advisors and to influence stakeholders, whether on agile or more traditional projects, has not disappeared. The same can be said for demands to balance distributed teams' needs for efficient and effective communication tools with organizations' needs for consistency and security. We see seven trends in the business analysis and project management fields as we move further into the 21st century.

1. *Continued enthusiasm for agile.* The agile bandwagon hardly seems to be abating. Whether or not organizations have really adopted agile, appetites for big, waterfall-type projects have diminished.

   The BA world is embracing agile, as demonstrated in the release of the *Agile Extension to the BABOK® Guide*, ver. 2. Version 3.0 of the BABOK includes an agile perspective, and we expect to see an agile practitioner subcertification for business analysts.

2. *Resurgence of use cases, particularly on agile projects.* While many traditional projects have favored the use case technique, we have noticed an upsurge in interest in and questions about use cases on agile projects. User stories, the most common format for writing agile requirements, are usually created at a high level of detail. Many agile teams are employing use cases to provide necessary detail.

3. *Focus on design.* Much of the BA's work includes fashioning solutions, so it is natural to think of this as design work. IIBA has given "design" an equal place at the business analysis table, describing design as "a usable representation of a solution."

4. *Increased use of the "cloud" and the need for business analysis in choosing cloud solutions.* Cloud computing will continue to have the allure of reducing investment in infrastructure and operations. The reality of needing to make information easily available to distributed team members will continue to trump data privacy concerns as teams increasingly use the cloud for storing and sharing project data.

   However, because of security concerns, organizations will align their security requirements to the potential cloud solution's security features; more analysis of overall requirements will be needed prior to investing in new cloud solutions. To maximize investment and achieve the greatest value, organizations will use business analysis to evaluate prospective cloud solutions.

5. *Less email, more connecting.* Lack of employee engagement and its associated costs are as significant for projects as they are for organizations at large. Many, if not most, projects use geographically distributed team members, which involves considerable obstacles to engagement. Business analysts will spend increasing time and effort to connect with stakeholders and team members. Fortunately, the availability of synchronous communication tools (audio and video) continues to grow.

6. *Focus on communicating first and documenting second.* Organizations are realizing that business analysts bring more value to the organization when they have exceptional skills to listen, observe, question, and probe for real needs rather than simply producing documentation. These skills must include the ability to influence stakeholders to understand and accept the recommended solution. Further, BAs must be able to communicate the results of their analysis to the stakeholders in a way that promotes understanding and gains acceptance and buy-in. Organizations will realize that communication targeted to the group or individual has greater impact than a voluminous requirements document.

7 *Focus on requirements management in project management.* The project management community is showing a greater interest in requirements activities. This can only be good for business analysts.

PUTTING IT ALL TOGETHER

WHAT DOES THIS MEAN FOR THE BUSINESS ANALYST?

There's no escaping the every-changing trends in business analysis. They will continue to evolve, and their implications—which will vary for different types of organizations—merit serious attention by BAs who aspire to work at the enterprise/strategic levels. Your challenge is to find your niche within a wide and transforming profession.

WHAT DOES THIS MEAN FOR THE BA MANAGER/PRACTICE LEAD?

As these and other trends take hold, BA managers/practice leads must prepare for the disruption of long-standing practices as well as the emergence of as-yet-unimagined business practices. These business and technology trends will not only provide opportunities for you to build a strong BA team, but will also open new avenues of application of BA principles and practices.

NOTES

1   IBM, "Actionable Business Architecture," online at *www-935.ibm.com/services/us/gbs/strategy/ actionable_business_architecture* (accessed March 2014).

2   Gartner: Top Ten Strategic Technology Trends for 2014. *Forbes Tech,* 10/14/2014. Online at: *www.forbes.com/sites/peterhigh/2013/10/14/gartner-top-10-strategic-technology-trends-for-2014* (accessed March 2014).

3   Jacques Bughin, Michael Chui, and James Manyika, "Ten IT-enabled Business Trends for the Decade Ahead," *McKinsey Quarterly,* May, 2013. Online at *www.mckinsey.com/insights/high_ tech_telecoms_internet/ten_it-enabled_business_trends_for_the_decade_ahead* (accessed March 2014).

Epilogue

couldn't resist the temptation to sneak in a personal word or two. The journey through the growth of both the business analysis and project management professions has been a gratifying one for me. During my trek I have had many inspiring and rewarding experiences presenting to groups at conferences and companies all over the world, from Ireland to Slovenia to New Zealand. I have also had the honor of consulting with CIOs, IT managers, PMOs, and BA practice leads across multiple industries, including pharmaceuticals, financial services, energy, healthcare, federal and state governments, and nonprofits. Consulting has afforded me the opportunity to peek inside multiple companies in diverse industries, uncovering invaluable insights.

I believe that business analysis is one of the most important, enjoyable, and satisfying professions, helping us navigate this chaotic, hyperconnected world. Especially as BAs become consultants instead of analysts, they will provide ever more value to their organizations. And, as we have emphasized throughout this book, it's all about value.

Perhaps one of the most heartwarming experiences I have had was seeing my son, Joey, follow in my footsteps. He is a project manager extraordinaire! After seeing me present at a project management conference, one of his colleagues asked him: "At exactly what age did your mother tell you that you had to become a project manager?"

One of the highlights of our sharing a career was when Joey invited me to conduct a two-day workshop for his project manager and business analysis peers. It was such a pleasure to see him in his element, with everyone teasing him and having fun. He introduced me by saying: "Welcome to the first annual 'bring your mommy to work' day." At one point during the session, when Joey and I were talking about the business value of IT, a person at the table told him to stop arguing with his mother. I had a little fun by inserting a few pictures of him as a toddler into my presentation, and someone shouted: "He still wears that sailor suit; I've seen him in it."

So it is fitting that I close with some words of wisdom from on the ground from Joey as he manages incredibly complex projects. Let's hear it for the next generation! It's your turn now.

A View from on the Ground

GREAT PROJECT MANAGERS

Joey Hass
Complex IT Project Manager
Insurance Industry

What makes *good* project managers *great* project leaders? Surprisingly, it's not about performance to schedule or budget; it's not even about delivering the full scope of the solution. These are important metrics to manage and monitor project delivery. However, what it really boils down to is building and sustaining strong relationships with two critical groups: customers and team members.

First, it's all about the customers. Build strong relationships with all customers involved in the project, internal and external, so that you truly represent the customers to the team when making critical decisions. Even better, involve the customers in your project as critical members of the team with a strong voice.

Second, take exceptional care of your team. Learn how to build, nurture, support, and sustain a high-performing team that gets things done. Great teams cannot be held back. Being part of a high-performing team is an amazing experience, and leading one is an absolute pleasure.

Unleashing the Potential of Your BA Practice

Sarah Gibson, CEO
Redvespa

Redvespa is an information technology company specializing in business analysis headquartered in Wellington, New Zealand. Redvespa's goal is to be the best, most fun, most professional, and easiest-to-work-with business analysis consultancy. From board level to the passionate CEO, Redvespa helps businesses make bold decisions and realize change through the power of business analysis. To become—and stay—the best, Redvespa pays attention to these elements of a great organization:

- Establish a positive culture to maximize positive impact.

- Become a purpose-driven organization.

- Create a lean organization and governance structure.

- Devise an inspirational brand.

- Take exceptional care of your people.

- Fiercely focus on learning and growth.

- Provide assessment tools that add value.

- Insist on creativity and innovation.

- Use communication as a tool to foster your values, spread your culture, and advertise your brand.

- Build and nurture a thriving community.

- Adopt integrated tools that set BAs free.

- Inspire your community of BA consultants.

- Celebrate!

ESTABLISH A POSITIVE CULTURE TO MAXIMIZE POSITIVE IMPACT

Do you want to generate great requirements or do you want to make a positive impact on your customers/partners/organization? The culture of business analysis teams differs greatly depending on the answer to that question. Organizational culture is *how we do things around here*. Positive cultures produce results. Deals are made. Innovative solutions are delivered. Value is added.

Redvespa spends a lot of time building a culture that puts our people and clients first. We work hard to find the right people, knowing that with the right people, amazing things can happen. Redvespa looks for talent with that special combination of analytical and people skills, and gives them the love (yes, love) and support they need to deliver for their clients and have fun in the process. Redvespa's people are great listeners and dynamic, with enquiring minds and sharp analytic skills. They are creative, professional, excellent communicators, and have the kinds of personalities that fit in virtually any environment.

BECOME A PURPOSE-DRIVEN ORGANIZATION

By defining and developing a core purpose for your BA practice group, you will create a framework for making decisions that will unleash your potential for creativity, initiative, and innovation. Uncover your BA practice team's unique purpose and ignite a vitality and commitment among your BAs and your customers alike.

Your purpose must be clearly defined, authentic, and aligned with business strategy. When strategically aligned and cleverly deployed, purpose enables meaningful engagement with all of your stakeholders, from employees to customers.

Knowing that becoming a purpose-driven enterprise is sound business and brand strategy, Redvespa used the Jim Collins approach to establish our core ideology, consisting of core purpose and values, and thus envision our future direction (*www.jimcollins.com*). Redvespa's core ideology is unique:

CORE IDEOLOGY
Core Purpose
We will make change happen to unleash potential and enrich people, business, and communities.
Core Values
Care—we care about people; we care for business **Vitality**—passion, energy, enthusiasm **Integrity**—honest, sincere, making tough calls, reliable **A Players**—it's all about attitude! innovative, creative, adaptable, motivated **Realism**—down to earth, authentic, genuine, what you see is what you get, pragmatic

CREATE A LEAN ORGANIZATION AND GOVERNANCE STRUCTURE

When setting up the optimal structure for your BA practice group, remember to be lean, efficient, and simple to traverse for all stakeholders. The structure of your BA center can help or hinder its progress toward accomplishing its goals. Strive to match your needs with the structure that is acceptable within your culture. Traditionally, we have accepted that there are three main types of organizational structures: functional, divisional, and matrix. However, the organizations of the future are much more fluid and open, with information flowing horizontally as well as vertically.

To set an optimal organization and governance structure in motion, Redvespa has designed a lean model to support the organization through its people to accomplish its purpose. The Redvespa organization consists of these main entities:

- Board

- CEO

- Two delivery centers

- Two key manager roles at each center:
  - o Delivery manager
  - o Business development manager

- BA consultants.

Redvespa has a board of advisors whose purpose is to add value to Redvespa through oversight, insight, and foresight. The board is responsible for:

- Setting strategy with the CEO and management team

- Monitoring performance toward achieving the strategy

- Supporting the CEO and acting as a sounding board, giving advice and assistance as needed.

The CEO leads the charge of Redvespa and is responsible for:

- Strategic and operational planning and implementation

- Financial management, people care and culture, establishing strategic partnerships

- Leading and contributing to international practices

- Setting priorities and signing off on the internal program of work.

Redvespa is based in two cities in New Zealand—Wellington and Auckland. The two cities have the same structure for caring for consultants and delivering to clients. Each location has a delivery manager (DM) and a business development manager (BDM).

The purpose of DMs is to love the consultants so they can delight the customers. They are responsible for:

- Leading and supporting all of Redvespa's consultant capability development

- Aligning consultant capability with market demand and strategy

- Monitoring delivery quality and managing escalation as appropriate

- Supporting consultants on client sites and delivering internal work assignments

- Rewarding and recognizing consultants

- Guiding professional development and performance enhancement, taking industry trends into account

- Managing the ideas and initiatives of Redvespa personnel

- In partnership with the BDM, recruiting all new consultants.

The purpose of BDMs is to delight Redvespa customers. They are responsible for:

- Achieving sales targets as agreed with the CEO

- Maintaining relationships with client organizations

- Determining market demand and identifying opportunities through client interactions

- Working closely with the delivery managers to monitor client satisfaction

- Maintaining relationships with consultants and prospective candidates

- Managing client contracts.

DEVISE AN INSPIRATIONAL BRAND

Most practice leads do not pay much attention to branding, but do not make that mistake. Branding is the consistent outward look projected by an organization. The BA practice brand needs to be an outgrowth of your corporate strategy, mission, image, and activities. Your brand will provide an image of the BA practice in the minds of all stakeholders and create a perception of what you stand for. Your branding strategy needs to be reflected throughout all communication, whether verbal or written. A branding strategy creates a guide for your BA team to follow to achieve a cohesive look for your team.

Redvespa has invested heavily in its brand, recognizing that branding is an important part of culture and facilitates building strong relationships among consultants and with clients. The Redvespa brand is one of its key differentiators and its mantra, "hell bent on delivery," says it all. We want our customers to see us taking action and placing high value on our relationships. We want our clients to be willing to invest in Redvespa because *we deliver.* The Redvespa brand consists of four elements:

Redvespa Brand Personality

- At ease with others

- Always relaxed in company

- A little bit quirky

- Like to create excitement, a buzz

- Cheeky, irreverent, and fun

Redvespa Brand Reflection

- Takes action

- Places high value on relationships

- Is willing to invest in alternatives that have consistently delivered

Redvespa Brand Self-Image

- Engage with people; truly connect

- Relate at both organizational and personal levels

- Take time to understand the issues and make the tough calls

- Always deliver

- Relationships have integrity

Redvespa Brand Culture

- Our heritage is as a Wellington company.

- We belong to global communities.

- We always push boundaries.

- We collaborate and contribute altruistically.

- We are non-traditionalist.

- We are kiwi—accessible, inclusive, generous, can-do attitude, and pioneering.

TAKE EXCEPTIONAL CARE OF YOUR PEOPLE

It is essential to demonstrate to your BA team that they are valued, cared for, and supported. Invest in, recognize, and reward your BAs. You might even consider referring to your BAs as *BA consultants*. Immediately, the role of the BA is elevated in most peoples' minds. Redvespa has developed a recognition guide and a reward guide, which cover multiple topics:

- Recognition: what it is, and what it is not

- Why recognition

- Relationship to recruitment, retention, capability enhancement

- Relationship to culture

- Performance reviews (Redvespa doesn't do them)

- The assignment lifecycle

- Post-project reviews for:

  o Consultant

  o Client

- Individual development plans

- Performance and pay.

FOCUS ON LEARNING AND GROWTH

You need to nurture, support, and develop your BA team with the right kind of learning and growth. Elements of a great BA development program include programs for high potential employees, succession planning, training, coaching, and mentoring.

All Redvespa employees are encouraged to seek opportunities for learning new skills and gaining new knowledge. These opportunities always align with Redvespa's strategic direction. Employees complete an education evaluation form after an event to evaluate learning opportunities.

PROVIDE ASSESSMENT TOOLS THAT ADD VALUE

Assess your BA capabilities against those in your industry to ensure that you have a world-class BA practice. Redvespa uses an assessment tool to measure and assess its BA consultants against a global benchmark. The assessment provides both individual and organizational capability information.

- The individual capability assessment results are used as a conversation starter and thought-provoker with consultants. The results lead to conversations about the consultants' skills and experiences, areas they may want to grow in, and areas we would like to see them develop.

- The business analyst capability assessment group report provides us with an overall assessment of the skills and competencies of consultants, evaluating capabilities against the complexity of projects as well as performance and project outcomes.

INSIST ON CREATIVITY AND INNOVATION

As you build your team of BA consultants, foster, encourage, and insist on an innovative mind set. Constantly ask the question: *Are we really innovating?*

At Redvespa, we have a program called *Bright Red Sparks*. It is designed to encourage all employees to share their great ideas for growing the organization—a new service or product, a tweak to processes, or a new avenue through which to market ourselves. Ideas can be submitted at any time by employees by completing a form explaining:

- What and why; description of the problem/opportunity

- Who it impacts

- Outcome; expected benefits.

Redvespa identifies a sponsor for each idea, who determines whether the submission contains enough information to assess whether it's worth taking forward. Every idea is considered against some basic criteria:

- Is it desirable (from a strategy, market and investment perspective)?

- Is it feasible (something we can deliver)?

- Is it viable (profitable and operational)?

USE COMMUNICATION AS A TOOL TO FOSTER YOUR VALUES, SPREAD YOUR CULTURE, AND ADVERTISE YOUR BRAND

Redvespa has developed a communications continuity plan. All communication strategies and tactics align with the purpose and core values of Redvespa. The plan includes brand-strategy journey communication, a thought leadership and leverage program, an awareness and engagement program, and opportunities for sponsorship relationships and event commitments. Currently Redvespa has two regular e-newsletters.

The internal newsletter, *Sidecar*, typically includes:

- An update from the CEO

- Important dates—internal events, IIBA events, training schedule

- Moovers and groovers—an update on where everyone is working these days

- Watch out for—Redvespa blog postings on the Redvespa website, in *BA Times*, and trends we've noticed

- What's cooking internally—updates on internal project work

- Surfing the net—interesting sites DMs have been reading (e.g., on design thinking, leadership trends, new tools and techniques)

- Education tune-up—education evaluations

- Events we're hosting—thought leaders/keynote speakers we're bringing to New Zealand

- Getting to know new people.

The external newsletter, *Buzz*, typically includes:

- What Redvespa is doing to add value—international speakers, training, the diagram book

- IIBA—What's happening?

- BA blogs and other social media

- Redvespa BA Leaders and Managers Forum update

- Redvespa Dancing on Tables—what are we celebrating?

BUILD AND NURTURE A THRIVING COMMUNITY

Build your community of BA consultants and their support team to continually sustain greatness. At Redvespa, we hold an annual two-day getaway event. The purpose is to get everyone in the business together, to have fun, share stories, laugh, and eat and drink together—and for everyone to learn something new, to share business strategies and goals, and to get inspired! The annual getaway is driven by the delivery management team, with logistic expertise from the business manager and support team. There's always a feedback form at the end of getaway so we can do better next time based on lessons learned.

Research and planning for the annual Redvespa gathering starts early in the new year. There is usually a theme and a "surprise and delight" approach, so there is an element of secrecy and anticipation. In previous years team activities have included making short films; shopping for, cooking, and serving a four-course meal in teams; and coming up with ideas to make a submission to *The B Team,* an organization dedicated to doing business better for people, planet, and profit.

ADOPT INTEGRATED TOOLS THAT SET BAs FREE

BAs without effective tools are at a huge disadvantage, spending inordinate amounts of time developing and maintaining documents and models. At some point, the documentation loses its efficacy and therefore its value to the organization. BA tools have grown up, and we need to adopt them to perform at our best.

Redvespa is tool-agnostic; we use what fits our purpose based on the client and project needs. One tool we use is *The BA Kit,* a cloud-based practice management tool we developed. *The BA Kit* assists in delivering consistency on projects and visibility to delivery managers of client and internal projects. The kit houses a suite of templates aligned to IIBA, along with tips and techniques to enhance usage of those templates.

INSPIRE YOUR COMMUNITY OF BA CONSULTANTS

A BA practice lead probably won't see *inspiration* in his/her job description. Make no mistake, it is a vital part of your leadership.

At Redvespa, we get inspiration from sources all around the world, from other industries, from the next generation, and from books, blogs, online forums, and our people and their extended families. We follow brand trends, management and leadership trends, design trends, architecture trends, and technology trends; all provide us with inspiration.

CELEBRATE!

At Redvespa, celebration is the glue that binds. The celebration of our 10th anniversary in 2013 was a wonderful opportunity to take stock of where we're at, where we're going, and acknowledge all the support, trust, guidance, and fabulous people we've met along the way. We've employed lots of wonderful new people, we've opened a new office, we've got loyal clients who advocate for us, and we've added BA capability service offerings. Most importantly, we have the most awesome celebratory parties. We really love what we do and we celebrate it regularly!

Sample Business Case

<Company name>

Value-Based Business Analysis Practice Implementation

Business Case

Version 1.0
Date Prepared:
Prepared by:

DOCUMENT CONTROL

	Information	
Document Owner	[Owner Name]	
Issue Date	[Date]	
Last Saved Date	[Date]	
File Name	[Name]	
Version	**Issue Date**	**Changes**
[1.0]	[Date]	[Section, Page(s) and Text Revised]

APPROVALS

Role	Name	Signature	Date

TABLE OF CONTENTS

1   EXECUTIVE SUMMARY

The purpose of this document is to present the case to establish < or improve, or transform> our business analysis practices at <company name>. This business case was authored by <insert name of author> in collaboration with:

- < name/title>

- < name/title>

- < name/title>

- < name/title>

<Be sure to include others in the development of the business case who are influential and represent other disciplines such as PM, IT management, business management, and accounting (to help with ROI.)>

A strong, effective, value-based business analysis practice is needed for us to significantly improve our return on project investments. Since we are dependent on complex IT-enabled projects to grow and remain competitive, we propose to use the discipline of business analysis to change the way we do projects to focus on *business value* and *innovation*.

While there are some world-class BA practices in existence, far too many attempts to implement a business analysis practice have been only marginally successful. Too often the improvements have been driven exclusively from the bottom up. While support is needed from all levels of the organization, grassroots efforts tend to be project-specific, disappearing gradually as project teams are disbanded. Therefore, we are recommending a holistic, top-down approach to implementation of a value-based BA practice.

2   BUSINESS VISION

<Describe the current situation, tailoring this entire section to your situation.>

2.1   BUSINESS NEED

<Company name> has recently centralized its business analysts, who were previously placed in various business units and in IT. The BAs are now part of <group>, which comprises multiple shared services including the PMO, IT training, the project services group, the vendor, and testing and program management offices. This centralization of business analysts was the first step in creating a value-based business analysis practice that is integrated with other project support disciplines.

2.2   CORE PURPOSE

The purpose of implementing a value-based BA practice is to enable <company name> to:

- Build the capabilities to optimize our business practices to execute strategy

- Transition our IT-enabled business projects from a focus on technology to a focus on business value

- Ensure that adequate enterprise/strategy analysis is conducted prior to building a business case for a proposed new project to ensure the business need is understood and the most innovative solution is proposed

- Increase our capability to elicit, analyze, prioritize, specify, and validate business requirements

- Validate the assumptions and forecasts made in the business case throughout the solution development phases to continuously confirm the case for continued investment

- Measure the business benefits of newly deployed business solutions

- Ensure that business benefits are achieved and technology is used as a competitive advantage

- Integrate the practices of business analysis with business architecture; business process; business rules and decisions; project, program, and portfolio management; and business strategy and transformation to build and sustain an organization that drives business/technology innovation.

2.3 CORE VALUES

The core values of the BA practice include the following:

- Collaboration – We are a team of BA consultants who work together with all project stakeholders to add value to our customers and wealth to the bottom line.

- Recognition – We will recognize the involvement of all project team members and strive to build high-performing project teams.

- Honesty and Integrity – We will build a team of BA consultants who are open, honest, knowledgeable, expert, and trustworthy.

- Innovation – We will foster creativity and innovation to consistently explore new ways of delivering value.

- Empowerment – We will foster critical thinking, problem-solving, and adaptability to enhance professional growth.

- Business Benefits – We will implement a decision-making process based on adding value to our customers and wealth to the bottom line.

2.4   ENVISIONED FUTURE

We envision a future business analysis practice that ensures that:

- Critical change initiatives realize the forecast business benefits (as documented in the project business case)

- Business analysis practices are transformed into a value-creating management tool

- Business analysts are viewed as respected consultants

- Technology is used as a competitive advantage.

3   STRATEGY

3.1   GOALS

<Develop/customize goals>

The goals of the business analysis practice include:

- Establishing clearly defined business analyst roles

- Developing a capable high-performing BA team

- Modernizing BA methods and tools

- Fostering creativity and innovation

- Delivering business benefits through projects in terms of:

o Value to our customers

o Wealth to the bottom line.

3.2 OBJECTIVES

<Develop/customize objectives>

The objectives of the business analysis practice are updated annually.

3.2.1 *Year 1*

- Secure executive approval of the BA practice implementation business case.

- Form governance structure (BA practice executive sponsor and steering/advisory committee).

- Appoint a BA practice lead.

- Establish a centralized BA team.

- Implement the initial infrastructure needed for the BA practice (soft implementation of a BA center of excellence, perhaps called a BA community of practice).

- Review BA staffing assignments to ensure that critical projects have appropriately skilled BAs.

- Ensure that critical projects have an approved business case and an executive sponsor.

- Establish BA role definition, required competencies, and career progression in alignment with best practices.

- Identify individual BA strengths and opportunities, accompanied by recommendations for learning and development.

- Assess the current state of BA practices and develop a plan to close the gaps.

- Initiate a BA professional development program.

- Initiate a BA communication program.

3.2.2 Year 2

- Implement a formal BA center of excellence.

- Integrate the practices of business analysis with business architecture; business process; business rules and decisions; project, program, and portfolio management; and business strategy and transformation to build and sustain an organization that drives business innovation.

- Augment the BA team to fill competency gaps with consultants/ mentors.

- Reassess the maturity of practices and capability of BAs and fill gaps.

3.2.3 Year 3

- Implement a formal balanced scorecard measurement system that is consistent with corporate performance reporting.

- Implement a strategic communications program.

- Develop a corps of enterprise/strategic level BA consultants.

- Develop an innovation program.

3.3 ALIGNMENT

This initiative will positively advance the following strategic and operational goals.

<List strategic and operational goals and describe how business analysis will contribute to their achievement.>

Relationship of BA Practice to <company name> Strategic Goals

Strategic Goal	The BA Practice Maturity Program will:

Relationship to <company name> Operational Goals

Operational Goal	The BA Practice Maturity Program will:

3.4 STAKEHOLDERS

<Identify/customize stakeholders>

The stakeholders involved in the implementation of a value-based BA practice are identified below. We will involve these individuals and groups in all critical decisions about the BA improvement effort.

Stakeholder Individual/ Group	Involvement / Role	Current Knowledge of Business Analysis (1 – 5)*	Affiliation with the BA Practice (1 – 5)* Importance (1 – 5)*	Support Needed -Not Needed -Helpful -Critical
Executives	• Support the BA practice • Support implementation of the BACOE • Communicate the value of the BA role			
Directors and mid-level managers in business units and in IT	• Fund and support the BACOE • Fund and support the implementation of the BA professional development program and recommendations to improve the BA practice • Communicate the value of the BA role			
BA supervisors and managers	• Participate in and support the BACOE • Support implementation of the BA professional development plan and recommendations to improve the BA practice • Communicate the value of the BA role			
Business analysts	• Participate in and support the BACOE • Participate in and support implementation of the BA professional development plan and improvements to the BA practice			

Stakeholder Individual/ Group	Involvement / Role	Current Knowledge of Business Analysis (1 – 5)*	Affiliation with the BA Practice (1 – 5)* Importance (1 – 5)*	Support Needed -Not Needed -Helpful -Critical
Project managers PMCOE	• Support advancement of the BA role • Communicate the value of the BA role • Elevate the BA to a leadership role on project teams			
BACOE	• Coordinate establishment of the BACOE • Develop BA practice 3-year strategic plan and annual business plan • Design and execute the BA professional development program • Implement the BA practice improvement recommendations			

Legend*

Current Level of Knowledge about Business Analysis	1 = Uninformed	2 = Basic	3 = Knows Key Concepts	4 = Knowledgeable	5 = Expert
Affiliation with BA Practices	1 = Antagonistic	2 = Resistant	3 = Neutral	4 = Supporter	5 = Ally
Importance of BA	1 = Irrelevant	2 = Neutral	3 = Relevant	4 = Very Relevant	5 = Essential

3.5   OPPORTUNITY ANALYSIS

<Update/customize>

The BA practice will be designed to solve business problems and seize valuable business opportunities.

3.5.1 Business Problem

Currently, executives, managers, and supervisors are only marginally aware of the value of enterprise/strategic business analysis practices as they relate to our strategy execution, innovation, value to customers, and wealth to the bottom line. The adverse impacts of this problem are felt by our BAs:

- We are struggling to implement business analysis practices from the bottom up in the absence of leadership from the top. The collective result is wasted resources, inadequate return on project investments, and loss of revenue as a result of failed and challenged projects.

- As individual business analysts strive to improve their BA performance, their efforts are only somewhat successful as a result of lack of organizational and managerial support.

3.5.2 Business Opportunity

The expected benefits include:

- Increased ability to understand and document the real business need

- A stronger focus on business value throughout the project lifecycle

- Agility to make course corrections as more is learned or business needs change

- Realization of business benefits from newly deployed solutions in terms of value to the customer and wealth to the organization

- Fewer failed and challenged projects

- Ability to execute strategy through project outcomes.

3.5.3 *Desired Outcome*

The desired outcome of this initiative is to:

- Understand the current state of our BA practice

- Understand the current level of our BA workforce capability

- Develop a BA practice maturity program and roadmap to close the gaps in both BA practices and BA workforce capabilities

- Measure the benefits of improved BA capability and practices

- Measure the business benefits realized from new solutions in terms of ROI of project investments, value to customers, and wealth to the bottom line.

4 CAPABILITY GAPS

4.1 CAPABILITIES OF OUR BA TEAM

A BA individual/workforce capability model is useful in determining the capabilities of our BA workforce. The model is designed to help us determine the level of BA capability that currently exists within our organization as well as the level of capability needed to successfully execute projects based on their complexity. From this information, we are able to identify the gaps in skills and competencies and draft a recommended BA learning and development plan. The model is four-tiered, with the levels of the model based on the escalating complexity of typical BA assignments.

Area of Focus	Business Outcomes
Operations and Support Focused Projects	Business operations are maintained and enhanced.
Project Focused Projects	Business objectives are met through projects.

Area of Focus	Business Outcomes
Enterprise Focused Projects	Business strategy is executed through projects, programs, and portfolios.
Competitive Focused Projects	New business strategy is forged and competitive advantage is improved through innovation and business/technology optimization.

Operations and Support Focus

To maintain and enhance business operations, both generalists and system specialists are needed. These BAs typically spend about 30 percent of their time doing business analysis activities for low to moderately complex projects designed to maintain and continually improve business processes and technology. The remaining time they are often fulfilling multiple roles, including developer, engineer, SME, domain expert, and tester. As legacy processes and systems age, these BAs are becoming more valuable since they are likely the best (and often the *only*) SMEs who understand the current business processes and supporting technology.

Project Focus

To ensure business objectives are met through projects, both IT- and business-oriented BAs are needed. These BAs work on moderately complex projects designed to develop new/changed business processes and IT systems. Competencies at this level encompass the skills needed to be successful at level 2 of the organizational practice maturity model.

- *IT-oriented PMs and BAs* improve operations through changes to technology. The BAs are mostly generalists, with specialists that include experience analyst, business rules analyst, business process analyst, and data analyst.

- *Business-oriented PMs and BAs* improve operations through changes to policy and procedures. Business-oriented PMs and BAs are mostly specialized, focused on finance, human resources, marketing, manufacturing, etc. In decentralized organizations, these PMs and BAs are dedicated to a major business area, improving the processes and the corresponding technologies used to run the operations. In more centralized organizations, these PMs and BAs are organized as a pool of talent whose efforts can be transferred seamlessly to the areas of the enterprise that are in most need of project support. Competencies at this level involve the skills needed to be successful at level 2 of the BA workforce capability model.

PM/BA Workforce Capability Model

Business Operations Enhanced	Business Objectives Met	Business Strategy Executed	New Business Strategy Forged
1. Operations Focus	**2. Project Focus**	**3. Enterprise Focus**	**4. Competitive Focus**
LOW COMPLEXITY PROJECTS	**MODERATELY COMPLEX PROJECTS**	**HIGHLY COMPLEX PROJECTS/PROGRAMS**	**BREAKTHROUGH INNOVATION PROJECTS**
OUTCOMES	OUTCOMES	OUTCOMES	OUTCOMES
Value of operational business process and systems is continually enhanced	Projects are managed to ensure new solutions meet business objectives	The enterprise is investing in the most valuable initiatives and is realizing the business benefits forecast in the business case	New strategy formulated, business/technology optimized, and competitive position improved
TYPE OF LEADER	TYPE OF LEADER	TYPE OF LEADER	TYPE OF LEADER
Generalists, business/system specialists, product managers	Business domain experts, IT system experts, product managers	Enterprise change experts, program and portfolio managers	Strategists, business/technology optimization experts, innovation and cultural change experts
Entry-level and senior PMs/BAs	Entry-level and senior PMs/BAs	Architects and enterprise BAs	
		Complex project, program, and portfolio managers	Innovators and strategists

Transition from Technical to Leadership Competencies
Continuous Advancement of Competence, Credibility, and Influence

©Kathleen Hass and Associates, 2012

Enterprise, Strategic Focus

At this level, BAs are trained and experienced in highly complex projects, programs, and portfolios. These BAs often specialize into two groups: enterprise analysts and business architects. They operate at the enterprise level of the organization, ensuring that the business analysis activities are dedicated to the most valuable initiatives and that business analysis artifacts (deliverables such as models and diagrams) are considered corporate assets and are therefore reusable. Enterprise BAs focus on the analysis needed to prepare a solid business case to propose new initiatives and work on highly complex enterprise-wide projects; business architects make the enterprise visible and keep the business and IT architectures in sync. Competencies at this level involve the skills needed to be successful at level 3 of the BA workforce capability model.

Competitive Focus

Competitive-focused BAs are business and technology visionaries who serve as innovation experts, organizational change specialists, and cross-domain experts. These BAs focus outside of the enterprise on what the industry is doing and design innovative new approaches to doing business to ensure the enterprise remains competitive or even leaps ahead of the competition. These BAs forge new strategies, translate strategy into breakthrough process and technology, and convert business opportunities into innovative business solutions. Competencies at this level involve the skills needed to be successful at level 4 of the BA workforce capability model.

Refer to Attachment 1, BA Workforce Capabilities and Techniques, for each level of the model to perform a quick informal assessment to identify capabilities that your BAs currently possess and demonstrate. Refer to the

IIBA *BABOK® Guide* for the detailed tasks performed for each competency area and techniques used to perform the work.

4.2 MATURITY OF OUR BA PRACTICES

Organizational maturity assessment frameworks are used to provide a standard and consistent method to determine the maturity of business practices for specific disciplines (e.g., business analysis, project management, software engineering). The BA practice maturity model is a four-stage model, with each stage representing a higher level of maturity. Foundational business analysis practices reside at level 2, whereas the more sophisticated BA practices that are needed to perform well on highly complex projects are at higher levels. The model also notes the many business management and leadership practices that are needed for successful project outcomes.

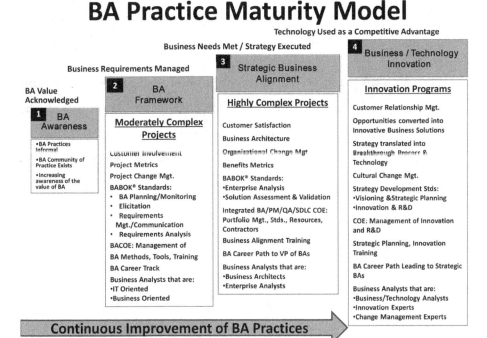

BA Practice Maturity Model

Technology Used as a Competitive Advantage

Business Needs Met / Strategy Executed

Business Requirements Managed

BA Value Acknowledged

1 BA Awareness

- •BA Practices Informal
- •BA Community of Practice Exists
- •Increasing awareness of the value of BA

2 BA Framework

Moderately Complex Projects

Customer Involvement
Project Metrics
Project Change Mgt.
BABOK® Standards:
- • BA Planning/Monitoring
- • Elicitation
- • Requirements Mgt./Communication
- • Requirements Analysis
BACOE: Management of BA Methods, Tools, Training
BA Career Track
Business Analysts that are:
- •IT Oriented
- •Business Oriented

3 Strategic Business Alignment

Highly Complex Projects

Customer Satisfaction
Business Architecture
Organizational Change Mgt
Benefits Metrics
BABOK® Standards:
- •Enterprise Analysis
- •Solution Assessment & Validation
Integrated BA/PM/QA/SDLC COE: Portfolio Mgt., Stds., Resources, Contractors
Business Alignment Training
BA Career Path to VP of BAs
Business Analysts that are:
- •Business Architects
- •Enterprise Analysts

4 Business / Technology Innovation

Innovation Programs

Customer Relationship Mgt.
Opportunities converted into Innovative Business Solutions
Strategy translated into Breakthrough Process & Technology
Cultural Change Mgt.
Strategy Development Stds:
- •Visioning &Strategic Planning
- •Innovation & R&D
COE: Management of Innovation and R&D
Strategic Planning, Innovation Training
BA Career Path Leading to Strategic BAs
Business Analysts that are:
- •Business/Technology Analysts
- •Innovation Experts
- •Change Management Experts

Continuous Improvement of BA Practices

©Kathleen Hass and Associates, 2012

— The BA practices required for each level are described in detail in Attachment 2, BA Practices at Each Level of Maturity. Perform a quick assessment and shade the practices that currently exist, are documented, and are performed on most projects.

5 APPROACH: BA PRACTICE IMPLEMENTATION AND SUSTAINABILITY

To implement and institutionalize a value-based BA practice, the business value that is promised needs to be fully understood across the organization, and BA benefits need to be continually demonstrated through measurement and communication programs. Leadership and sponsorship of the effort should emanate from the top of the organization and flow down to all levels. A holistic and methodical implementation approach and framework is fundamental to success and sustainability. Mature BA practices have several components: a capable BA team, organizational support, executive leadership, and sponsorship.

Typically, a BA practice is supported by a number of integrated elements that comprise a holistic framework as depicted below. To deal with the significant amount of change required by all project stakeholders, the BA practice implementation will be managed in three phases. See Attachment 3 for a detailed description of the phases of the framework.

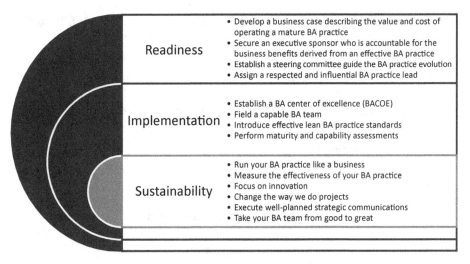

BA Practice Implementation Framework

5.1   INITIAL READINESS PHASE, ANSWERS THE QUESTION: "IS OUR ORGANIZATION READY?"

- The business case describing the value and cost of implementing a mature BA practice

- An executive sponsor who is accountable for the business benefits derived from an effective BA practice

- A steering committee to guide the BA practice evolution

- A respected and influential BA practice lead

5.2   SUBSEQUENT IMPLEMENTATION PHASE, ANSWERS THE QUESTION: "HOW DO WE BUILD THE BA PRACTICE?"

- The BA center of excellence

- A capable BA team

- Effective lean BA practice standards.

5.3 ONGOING SUSTAINABILITY PHASE, ANSWERS THE QUESTION: "HOW DO WE INSTITUTIONALIZE AND CONTINUE TO IMPROVE BA PRACTICES?"

- Run your BA practice like a business

- Measure the effectiveness of your BA practice

- Focus on innovation

- Change the way we do projects

- Execute well-planned strategic communications

- Take your BA team from good to great.

6 RETURN ON INVESTMENT IN BUSINESS ANALYSIS CAPABILITIES

6.1 PROJECT PERFORMANCE GOALS

Assuming improvements are in process for other key project delivery disciplines (e.g., project management, testing, QA, SDLC, vendor management), we can expect significant benefits to project performance. We suggest augmenting our current measurement program to collect metrics for the categories listed below.

Project Performance Goals	Current Performance	Performance Goals
1. Cost: on budget		
2. Duration: on schedule		
3. Scope: full set of functions and features		
4. Productivity: Number of projects completed without the need for additional resources		
5. Quality of deliverables: Reduced defects and rework		

Project Performance Goals	Current Performance	Performance Goals
6. Customer satisfaction		
7. Team performance		
8. Business Benefits: value to customer		
9. Business Benefits: wealth to bottom line		

6.2   BUSINESS ANALYSIS PERFORMANCE GOALS

We propose establishing goals and tracking the following information for each significant project that has a highly capable business analyst working throughout the project to measure return on BA investment.

BA Performance Goals	Current Performance	Performance Goals
Business Case Development Development of the business case is led by a senior BA who facilitated a group of experts (minimally, a senior PM, architect, business visionary, financial analyst).		
Business Case Validation Business case is updated at key milestones: BA validates assumptions and forecasts made in the business case; updates with new information; and presents results to executive sponsor with recommendation to continue investment or implement a course correction to achieve cost and benefit forecasts.		
Business Benefits Measured BA measures actual business benefits realized after the new/changed business solution is deployed vs. costs and benefits forecast in the business case.		
Root Cause Analysis Performed BA performs root cause analysis if forecast business benefits are not realized and recommends corrective action to process/decision-making to avoid in the future.		

BA Performance Goals	Current Performance	Performance Goals
Customer Value Actual customer value is measured by BA after the new solution is deployed and compared to the value forecast in the business case. If actual value is not achieved, BA makes recommendations to improve the solution to improve business outcomes. Customer satisfaction is continually improved.		
Team performance Team satisfaction is continually improved.		

6.3 ESTIMATED BENEFITS

<Be sure to list the specific projects the BA practice will initially support, and base benefit and cost estimates on those projects. If the projects do not have a business case estimating costs and benefits, develop one and secure approval from the project sponsor. The benefit estimates should be derived from a sum of the benefits projected for the specific projects. Estimates and assumptions/goals are provided below as sample data only.>

Benefits projected are based on the following projects that will be supported by the BACOE:

- Xxx

- Xxx

- Xxx.

Category	Benefit	Value	Assumptions/Goals	How We Will Measure
Financial	• New revenue generated • Increased profit margin	$x $x $x	• Achieve or exceed revenue benefits projected in business case	
Operational	• Improved operational efficiency • Reduction in product time to market • Enhanced quality of product/service • Reduction in costs	x % x hrs x %	• Achieve or exceed cost estimates projected in business case • Reduce rework by 40% • Reduce defects found after release by 40% • Reduce project time overruns by 50% • Reduce project cost overruns by 30%	
Market	• Increased market awareness • Greater market share • Additional competitive advantage	x % x % Describe	• Increase market share by 15% • Elevate competitive position by XXX	
Customer	• Improved customer satisfaction • Increased customer retention • Greater customer loyalty	x % x % Describe	• Increase customer satisfaction by 15% • Increase customer retention rate by 15%	
Employees	• Increased staff satisfaction • Improved organizational culture • Longer staff retention	x % Describe x %	• Increase project staff satisfaction by 15% • Increase project staff retention by 15%	

6.4 ESTIMATED COSTS

When fully implemented during year 2, the BA practice organization structure will likely resemble the following. Note that a single individual may fill more than one manager role depending on the number and complexity of projects that are supported.

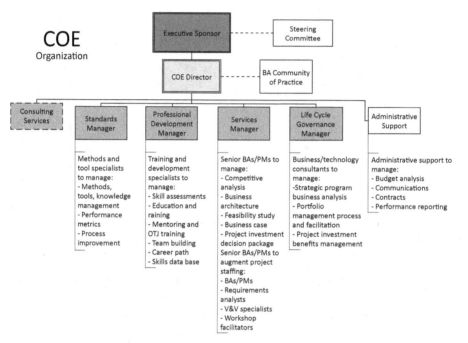

Category	Cost	Value / Year	Assumptions
People	• Salaries of BACOE staff • Contractors / outsourced parties • Training	$x $x $x	• BACOE staff of 3 senior-level • Team of BAs = 10
Physical	• Space for BACOE team • Equipment and materials • Tools (computers, phones, etc.)	$x $x $x	• Co-locate BACOE team • Co-locate BAs

Category	Cost	Value / Year	Assumptions
Marketing	• Advertising/branding/ website • Promotional materials • PR and communications	$ x $ x $ x	• Manage BACOE like a business • Brand BA practice • Develop Communications Plan
Organizational	• Operational down-time during implementation • Short-term loss in productivity • Cultural change management	$ x $ x *Describe*	• Develop Change Management Plan • Cultural change will initially involve costs

ATTACHMENT 1: BA WORKFORCE CAPABILITIES AND TECHNIQUES FOR EACH LEVEL OF BA

The capabilities that are included in the individual and workforce capability models consist of technical skills, supporting leadership and soft skill competencies, and techniques used to carry out the BA work. See below for a listing of capabilities required for each level of the model:

6.5   BA TECHNICAL COMPETENCY AREAS

Project-Focused:

- Business Analysis Planning and Monitoring
- Elicitation
- Requirements Management and Communication
- Requirements Analysis.

Enterprise-Focused:

- Enterprise Analysis
- Solution Assessment and Validation.

Competitive-Focused:

- Strategy Formation
- Creativity and Innovation
- Competitive Analysis.

Breakthrough Process and Product Design

6.6 BA TECHNIQUES USED TO PERFORM THE WORK

Operations/Support-Focused Business Analyst

1. Acceptance and Evaluation Criteria Definition
2. Brainstorming
3. Checklists
4. Continuous Process Improvement
5. Defect and Issue Reporting
6. Document Analysis
7. Estimation
8. Functional Decomposition
9. Interface Analysis
10. Interviews
11. Non-Functional Requirements Analysis
12. Observation
13. Problem Tracking
14. Replanning
15. Requirements Change Management
16. Requirements Documentation
17. Requirements Prioritization
18. Sequence Diagramming
19. Stakeholder Analysis/Mapping
20. Time Boxing / Budgeting
21. Voting

Project-Focused Business Analyst

1. Baselining
2. Business Case Validation
3. Business Process Analysis and Management
4. Business Rules Analysis and Management
5. Change Management
6. Conflict and Issue Management
7. Consensus Mapping
22. Requirements Briefings and Presentations
23. Requirements for Vendor Selection
24. Requirements Traceability/Coverage Matrix
25. Requirements Decomposition
26. Requirements Workshops
27. Requirements Review, Validation, and Signoff

8. Communications Requirements Analysis
9. Business Process Design
10. Data Dictionary and Glossary
11. Data Flow Diagrams
12. Data Modelling
13. Decision Analysis
14. Delphi
15. Expert Judgment
16. Focus Groups
17. Force Field Analysis
18. MoSCoW Analysis
19. Process Modelling
20. Prototyping
21. Requirements Attribute Assignment

28. Responsibility Matrix (RACI)
29. Reverse Engineering
30. RFI, RFQ, RFP
31. Risk Analysis
32. Scenarios and Use Cases
33. Scope Modelling
34. Solution Modelling
35. State Diagrams
36. Structured Walkthroughs
37. Survey/Questionnaire
38. User Acceptance Testing
39. User Stories and Storyboards
40. Value Analysis
41. Variance Analysis
42. Vendor Assessment

Enterprise-Focused Business Analyst

1. Balanced Scorecard
2. Benchmarking
3. Business Architecture
4. Business Case Development and Validation
5. Business Opportunity Analysis
6. Business Problem Analysis
7. Business Process Reengineering
8. Competitive Analysis
9. Cost/Benefit Analysis and Economic Modelling
10. Current State Analysis
11. Feasibility Analysis

12. Future State Analysis
13. Goal Decomposition
14. Gap Analysis
15. Last Responsible Moment Decision-Making
16. Lessons Learned Process
17. Metrics and Key Performance Indicators
18. Organizational Modelling
19. Organizational Change
20. Portfolio Analysis
21. Project and Program Prioritization
22. Root Cause Analysis (Fishbone Diagram)
23. SWOT Analysis

Competitive-Focused Business Analyst

1. Breakthrough Process Design
2. Cultural Change
3. Divergent Thinking
4. Edge-of-Chaos Analysis

10. Intuition
11. Investigation and Experimentation
12. Metaphors and Storytelling
13. Mind Mapping

5. Emotional Intelligence
6. Experimentation
7. Idea Generation
8. Innovation and Creativity
9. Innovation Teams

14. Pattern Discovery
15. Research and Development
16. Strategic Planning
17. Systematic Inventive Thinking
18. Visualization

ATTACHMENT 2: BA PRACTICES AT EACH LEVEL OF MATURITY

	Level 1 BA Awareness	Level 2 BA Framework	Level 3 Business Alignment	Level 4 Business/Technology Optimization
Business Outcomes Practices	**BA Value Acknowledged**	**Business Requirements Managed**	**Business Needs Met Strategy Executed**	**Technology used as a Competitive Advantage New Strategy Forged**
Customer Relationship Management		Customers and stakeholders are involved throughout the project.	Customer satisfaction is measured for both the process used to involve customers and the new business solution delivered by the project.	External customer relationships are measured and managed to continually increase customer satisfaction.
Standards, Methodology, Tools, Knowledge Management, Change Management	Process and tool standards are undefined.	• BA standards for practices and tools are defined and integrated. • Project knowledge is accessible to all project stakeholders. • Project scope changes are managed.	• BA standards, tools, and knowledge mgt. are integrated with PM, QA, SDLC standards • Organizational readiness assessments are conducted prior to deployment of new solutions.	• Convert business opportunities into innovative business solutions. • Translate strategy into breakthrough process and technology change. • Benchmarking, competitive analysis, feasibility analysis is conducted as part of the strategic planning process. • Cultural readiness assessments are conducted prior to deployment of new solutions.

	Level 1 BA Awareness	Level 2 BA Framework	Level 3 Business Alignment	Level 4 Business/Technology Optimization
Body of Knowledge Areas		Standards for the following knowledge areas are defined, institutionalized, and measured: • BA planning and monitoring • Elicitation • Requirements management and communication • Requirements analysis	Standards for the following knowledge areas are defined, institutionalized, and measured: • Enterprise analysis • solution Assessment and validation	
Project Selection and Prioritization			• The business and technology architectures are defined and in sync. • The portfolio management process ensures business alignment of projects.	
Metrics		• Project metrics for cost, time, and scope are collected, analyzed, and reported. • Requirement defects are tracked and measured; steps are taken for prevention in the future.	• Quantitative BA process management program exists and is integrated with PM, QA, SDLC • Business benefits management program is defined and in place.	Business benefits management program is tied to the portfolio management program.
Practice Support and Governance	BA forum or community of practice exists.	BACOE: Centralized management of BA Framework	BACOE: Centralized management of: • Business case development, portfolio management, BPM, BDM • Resources, contractors, vendors • Governance committee	BACOE: • Integrated with PM, QA, SDLC COEs • Centralized management of innovation and R&D

	Level 1 BA Awareness	Level 2 BA Framework	Level 3 Business Alignment	Level 4 Business/Technology Optimization
Training and Support		BA framework training program exists and all BAs attend.	• Business alignment training program exists and all BAs attend.	• Business/technology optimization training program exists and all BAs attend. • BA Training ROI is measured.
Competency and Career Development		BA career track exists for: • IT-oriented analysts • Business -oriented analysts	BA career path leading to VP business analysis exists for: • Business architecture analysts • Enterprise business analysts	BA career path leading to strategic and domain expert BAs exists for: • Business/technology analysts • Cross-functional analysts • Cross-domain analysts • Organizational change analysts • Innovation analysts

ATTACHMENT 3: IMPLEMENTATION FRAMEWORK

6.7   THE INITIAL READINESS PHASE

6.7.1   *The Business Case for a Mature BA Practice*

Many elements must be in place for you to declare your readiness to begin to implement a BA practice. The most important tool for you to present your argument for a mature BA practice is the business case.

Unless your BA practice can demonstrate results in business benefits in terms of value to the customer and/or wealth to the bottom line, it is a failed venture. Without a business case, you are likely engaged in steering a rudderless vessel. Developing the business case will enable you to think about all important aspects of the venture. Your BA practice business case must be convincing, compelling, and believable.

6.7.2   The Executive Sponsor

Once you have developed the business case to implement a BA practice, enlist an executive sponsor to guide the effort, to own the budget for the BA practice, and to commit to the cost and benefit projections. Usually, the executive sponsor is a very senior-level executive, such as the CIO or CSO (chief strategy officer).

6.7.3   The Executive Steering Committee

It is ideal to secure the approval of the experts who helped build the business case to serve on a BA practice steering committee. The steering committee, facilitated by the BA practice lead and chaired by the executive sponsor, will provide political cover, decision support, budget, and legitimacy to the BA practice initiative.

6.7.4   A Respected and Influential BA Practice Lead

Building a new business process such as business analysis is a challenging endeavor. Your initial trial is to gain executive confidence and organizational alignment up front. Do you have the power and influence skills to take a comprehensive view that is aligned with your environment, your culture, your strategies, and decision-making practices?

6.8   THE IMPLEMENTATION PHASE

6.8.1   A Home for the BA Practice: The BA Center of Excellence

The BA practice needs a home, a department that is accountable and responsible for building and sustaining effective BA practices. This center, which should be small (too large is deadly), is authorized to manage the

BA team; the business case process; organizational BA standards and frameworks; methods; training; tools, templates, and techniques; metrics; and communication.

6.8.2   A Capable BA Team

Today, BAs are mostly project-focused, creating and managing requirement artifacts. However, to become a valuable corporate asset, BAs need to become holistic thinkers who are strategically focused, concentrating on innovative solutions to complex business problems.

6.8.3   Effective Lean BA Practice Standards

In days gone by, we always followed the maxim, *process first, then tools*. The good news is that BA tools have grown up. Good BA standards are now embedded in integrated requirements management tools. So the tool helps educate BAs on the best practices, integrates and manages the requirements knowledge and artifacts, and helps forward engineer information into BA artifacts used to build the solution.

The bad news is most BAs still use desktop tools that are difficult to maintain and are disintegrated. As a result, the BA is burdened with creating, maintaining, integrating, and synchronizing all of the business strategies, goals, models, documents, matrices, use cases, user stories, test cases, etc. Adopt sophisticated tools to maintain reusable requirement artifacts, impose standards, and enable education of your BA team.

6.8.4   Maturity and Capability Assessments

It is often said that we don't need to do a maturity assessment because we know our capabilities are immature. The problem is, just knowing your capabilities are immature is not *actionable*. Assessments provide useful information about strengths, as well as gaps that need immediate improvement to grow to the next level of maturity. Assessments shed light on exactly where you are, provide a step-by-step improvement roadmap, and facilitate continuous improvements based on proven maturity models.

6.9 THE SUSTAINABILITY PHASE

6.9.1 *Run Your BA Practice like a Business*

Measurement is a key component of any new business area. Make no mistake; implementing a mature BA practice is no small endeavor. The effort is fraught with challenges. Targeted measurements and effective communications tailored to the needs of each stakeholder group are essential. The messages need to demonstrate the real business value brought about by improvement BA practices.

6.9.2 *Measure the Effectiveness of your BA Practice*

Continually increase the capabilities of your BA team and the maturity of your BA practice and boast of your progress throughout your organization. Measure the business benefits of your BA practice and of projects in terms of value to your customers and wealth to the bottom line. Demonstrate value through performance measures that tie to your organization's corporate scorecard.

6.9.3 *Focus on Innovation*

In this complex global economy, your organizational change initiatives need to result in innovative solutions; incremental changes to "business as usual" are no longer enough for organizations to remain competitive.

Yet, many CEOs do not believe they have the creative leadership needed to capitalize on complexity to bring about innovation.

So what does innovation have to do with business analysis? For BAs to reach their full potential and add the most value to their organizations, they must become *creative leaders of innovative change.* Traditional BA activities are still important, but a new focus on innovation is the 21st century call to action.

6.9.4   Change the Way we do Projects

An organization's culture is durable because it is "the way we do things around here." Changing the way it selects projects, develops and manages requirements, and manages projects, while focusing not only on business value but also on innovation, is likely a significant shift for an organization. Even today, many organizational cultures still promote the practice of piling project requests, accompanied by sparse requirements, onto the IT and new-product development groups and then wondering why they cannot seem to deliver.

6.9.5   Execute Strategic Communications

Use strategic communications as your most effective tool to ensure you realize the full value of your BA practice, and your organization knows it. Since project sponsors seldom measure accurately and then communicate the value derived from project and program solutions, the BA practice lead ensures these data are captured and shouted far and wide. An effective BA practice focuses primarily on business value, the true measure of project management and business analysis effectiveness. For the BA practice lead to be taken seriously and looked upon as a credible leader of change, she must engage in strategic communications. This involves:

- Thinking strategically, holistically, and systematically

- Crafting powerful messages that are impactful and memorable

- Influencing positive decision-making through intentional and targeted strategic communication.

6.9.6   *Take your BA Team from Good to Great*

Complex projects are challenged today because of people failing to come together with a common vision, an understanding of complexity, and the right expertise. Virtually all work today is accomplished by teams of people. Sometimes teams of teams consisting of groups around the globe. Team leadership is different from traditional management, and teams are different from operational work groups. When leading high-performing, creative teams, it is no longer about command and control; it is rather about collaboration, consensus, empowerment, confidence, and leadership.

APPENDIX B
Innovation Process Checklist

Using an expert team consisting of influential individuals who represent senior leaders and other key players (project manager, business visionary, product specialists, architect, and lead technologist), perform an assessment and opportunity selection.

1. Strategy Assessment

1.1 Review your organization's strategic plans, goals, and objectives.

- If the strategic goals have not been decomposed into specific objectives, convene a small expert team to do so.
- Look for new goals/objectives/opportunities. Use creativity techniques to "think out of the organization."
- Validate the strategy, goals, objectives, and opportunities with the appropriate senior executive(s).

1.2 Determine which objectives/opportunities have not been met.

1.3 Determine if a project/program is underway for unmet objectives/opportunities.

1.4 Prioritize objectives/opportunities that have not been addressed according to level of innovation and value of expected business benefits.

1.5 Develop a corporate scorecard for all unmet objectives/opportunities.

2. Internal Current-State Assessment

2.1 Assess your organization's internal environment (process, organization, locations, data, applications, technology, project/program/portfolio management, business analysis).

2.2 What problems or opportunities have not yet been addressed? Focus on:
- Processes that touch the customer
- Opportunities to innovate the value chain (processes that flow value through your organization to your customers) with breakthrough solutions.

2.3 What strategic goals/objectives are being hindered because problems/opportunities have not been addressed? What strategic objectives can be advanced if the problems/opportunities are addressed?

2.4 For the unaddressed problems/opportunities, what barriers have prevented solving the problems or seizing the opportunities?

2.5 What will determine when it is time to solve the problems?

2.6 Assuming the time is right, select the aspects of the business that need to be changed. (Key criterion: There is an opportunity to achieve unmet strategic goals/objectives through innovation.)

2.7 Define the opportunity you have to innovate to make a significant difference to your company:
- State the opportunity/problem.
- Identity all potential solutions using creative brainstorming techniques.
- Examine the feasibility of each option.
- Describe the most innovative solution option.
- Describe how the solution will bring about significant innovation, leading to a stronger competitive position in the marketplace.

2.8 What success criteria will ensure that you have addressed the issue through innovation and significantly improved your competitive position? What is the expected value in terms of business benefits?

2.9 How will you monitor progress to make sure the problem will remain solved or the opportunity will remain positive over time?

2.10 Develop a corporate scorecard for all high-value problems/opportunities to achieve unmet strategic goals/objectives through innovation.

3. External Current-State Assessment

3.1 Assess your organization's external environment (well-known competitors, start-ups, recent failed product or service introductions, demand for your current product line, pent-up or unspoken demand for innovative products/services).

3.2 What opportunities do you have to create something new, innovate, and disrupt the current competitive positioning in your favor?

3.3 What strategic goals/objectives are being hindered because the opportunities have not been pursued? Which strategic goals/objectives will be advanced?

3.4 What has stopped you from pursuing the opportunities?

3.5 What will determine when it is time to pursue the opportunities?

3.6 Rank opportunities according to level of innovation and potential business value. Select the highest value opportunities that advance strategies.

3.7 Define the opportunity you have to innovate to make a significant difference to your company:

- Identity all potential solutions using creative brainstorming techniques.
- Examine the feasibility of each option.
- Describe the most innovative solution option.
- Describe how the solution will result in breakthrough innovation, leading to a significantly stronger competitive position in the marketplace.

3.8 What success criteria will ensure that you have seized the opportunity through innovation? What is the expected value in terms of business benefits?

3.9 How will you monitor progress to make sure that the problem will remain solved or the opportunity will remain positive over time?

3.10 Develop a corporate scorecard for the most innovative and highest value opportunities.

---

4. Opportunity Selection

Select from among the opportunities identified during the assessments. Facilitate the group to reach agreement on a high-level plan for closing the gaps between the current state and the future vision.

4.1 Rank all identified opportunities based on expected level of innovation and business benefit.

4.2 Conduct a feasibility analysis for the top-priority opportunities. Assess the following aspects of feasibility:

- Economic feasibility: Can we afford to invest in the opportunity?
- Time-to-market feasibility: Can we meet the market window in time to disrupt the current competitive positioning and leap ahead?
- Commercial change feasibility: Can we manage the groundbreaking commercial practices?

- Organizational change feasibility: Can we manage the organizational changes needed to support the new product/service?
- Level of exposure feasibility: Can we meet regulatory and other environmental constraints?
- Technological feasibility: Does the technology exist and is it proven?
- Knowledge and skill feasibility: Do we have, or can we quickly acquire, the knowledge, skills, and expertise we need to field the innovation team?
- Clarity feasibility: Is the opportunity clear and unambiguous; is the solution defined and achievable?
- Requirements feasibility: Are requirements understood and unambiguous?
- Political feasibility: Can we secure management approval of the groundbreaking innovation?
- Market feasibility: Will people in our target market embrace the new product or service?

4.4 Select the most feasible opportunity and build the business case.

About the Contributors

Michael Augello
BA Practice Consultant and Entrepreneur
michael.augello@iinet.net.au

Michael has extensive experience performing various consultant roles, including both operational and executive leadership. As co-founder and principal of a startup IT and BA consultancy, he led client relationship, sales, marketing, recruitment, staff care, delivery, and practice management activities. As an industry leader in business analysis, Michael now devotes his time to coaching and mentoring. He is a member of the IIBA board of directors, chairing the IIBA board nominations committee.

Andrea Brockmeier, PMP
Director of Project Management
Watermark Learning
andrea.brockmeier@watermarklearning.com
@afbrockmeier (Twitter)

Andrea has over 20 years of experience in project management practice and training. She writes and teaches courses in project management, including PMP® certification and influencing skills. She is actively involved with the PMI chapter in Minnesota, where she has been a member of the certification team for many years. Andrea regularly contributes articles on project management *to Project Times* and *Projects@Work*. She is particularly interested in the dynamics of global, virtual teams.

Barbara Carkenord, CBAP, MBA, PMP
Director of Business Analysis Practice
RMC Project Management
bcarkenord@rmcproject.com

Barbara is an author, presenter, and trainer. Her books include *Seven Steps to Mastering Business Analysis, CBAP/CCBA Exam Prep*, and *Managing Business Analysts*. Barbara also teaches business analysis professional skills and delivers presentations at industry conferences and professional association chapter events. She was a core writing team member of IIBA's *Business Analysis Guide to the Body of Knowledge* version 2.0 and contributed to development of the outline for version 3.0, focusing on the requirements analysis knowledge area and supporting development of the new BA framework.

Sarah Gibson, CEO
Redvespa
Sarah.Gibson@Redvespa.com

As CEO of Redvespa Consultants Limited, an IT consultancy specializing in business analysis, Sarah is primarily responsible for strategic and operational planning, people care, and culture and financial management. She is a member of the IIBA board of directors and past president of the New Zealand IIBA chapter. One of her goals is raising the profile of the BA profession in New Zealand and throughout the world.

Kate Gwynne, CBAP, CSM
Associate Director, Business Analysis
RESOURCE
KGwynne@Resource.com

With more than 20 years of experience helping organizations successfully align and implement their business and IT initiatives, Kate is a recognized leader in the Central Ohio analyst community. She specializes in building BA practices and centers of excellence, developing corporate training programs, and implementing initiatives to help reduce project rework and improve collaboration. Kate is a former board member of The Society for Marketing Professional Services and has been a guest speaker at various IIBA events and conferences.

Joey Hass, PMP, CSM
Complex Project Leader
joeyjams73@gmail.com

Joey is a seasoned, award-winning project leader who leverages his expertise and experience to steer complex projects through technology and cultural challenges. He has managed projects across industries as a consultant for major corporations and as an internal project manager for several leading insurance companies. He recently managed the complex IT integration following an acquisition for a major insurance company in half the expected time. Joey is the recipient of two leadership awards, the Silver Star award and the Winners Circle Leadership Excellence award.

Vicki James, PMP, CBAP
Director of Business Analysis
Watermark Learning
vicki.james@watermarklearning.com
@VickiPPS (Twitter)

Vicki has more than 15 years of experience in the public and private sectors as a project manager, business analyst, author, and independent industry consultant and trainer. She is co-author of *Strategies for Project Sponsorship* and a contributor to *The Complete Project Manager*. Vicki is currently president of the IIBA Seattle chapter and a past vice president of the PMI Olympia chapter.

Elizabeth Larson, PMP, CBAP, CSM
Co-principal and CEO
Watermark Learning
elizabeth.larson@watermarklearning.com
@e_larson (Twitter)

Elizabeth has over 30 years of experience in project management and business analysis. She and her husband Richard have co-authored the *CBAP Certification Study Guide, Practitioners' Guide to Requirements Management,* and *The Influencing Formula*. She has also co-authored articles that appear regularly in *BA Times, Project Times,* and *Modern Analyst*. Elizabeth was a lead contributor/expert reviewer to the *BABOK® Guide* versions 2.0 and 3.0 and a lead author/content lead for the *PMBOK® Guide,* fourth and fifth editions.

Richard Larson, PMP, CBAP
President and Founder
Watermark Learning
richard.larson@watermarklearning.com
@Rich_Larson (Twitter)

Richard has over 30 years of experience in business analysis, project management, training, and consulting. He and his wife Elizabeth have co-authored the *CBAP Certification Study Guide, Practitioners' Guide to Requirements Management,* and *The Influencing Formula.* He has also co-authored articles that appear regularly in *BA Times, Project Times,* and *Modern Analyst.* Richard has contributed to the *BABOK® Guide* version 2.0 and was a lead author on version 3.0 as well as a lead author on the *PMBOK® Guide,* fourth edition.

Michele Maritato, MBA, CBAP, PMP, PMI-RMP
PMProgetti Srl
www.pm-progetti.it

Michele has over 20 years of experience in business analysis and project management consulting for corporate reorganization programs, process re-engineering initiatives, and development of information systems and intelligent networks in several business sectors. He is director of IIBA and vice president for education and training of the IIBA Italy chapter and vice president of the PMI northern Italy chapter.

Roxanne Miller, CBAP
President and Founder
Requirements Quest®
roxanne@requirementsquest.com
@ReqSuperFreak (Twitter)

Roxanne is an author, speaker, requirements engineer, trainer, business analyst coach, and practitioner as well as a self-proclaimed "requirements super freak." As founder and president of Requirements Quest®, she consults on requirements management process improvement and business analysis practices. Roxanne is a frequent keynote speaker and workshop presenter at BA conferences across the globe. An active member and advocate for IIBA, she served as president of the IIBA greater Madison chapter. She helped Wisconsin IIBA chapters unite and co-founded an annual Wisconsin Business Analyst Development Day (WI BADD®), which is devoted to education, development, and networking opportunities for business analysis professionals. Roxanne is the author of *The Quest for Software Requirements*.

Sandra Sears, CCP, PMP
sls83@cornell.edu

An executive at a large insurance company, Sandra is responsible for IT process and practice development and has been a key player in a large IT transformation effort, leading the rollout of project management, business analysis, and testing practices and tools across the organization. Previously, she led the development of standardized processes for project portfolio management, IT financial management, and the solution delivery life cycle. At a previous company, she was the recipient of the prestigious Chairman's

Award for her work in introducing a new annuity product line in Tokyo. She has been a speaker at industry conferences for professional and educational organizations and an adjunct professor of computer sciences.

Index